# FIRST STEPS IN THE KINGDOM:

## A BELIEVER'S GUIDE TO UNDERSTANDING THEIR NEW LIFE WITH CHRIST

ERIC KOUASSI

authorHOUSE

*AuthorHouse*™
*1663 Liberty Drive*
*Bloomington, IN 47403*
*www.authorhouse.com*
*Phone: 833-262-8899*

*Published by AuthorHouse  04/18/2024*

*ISBN: 979-8-8230-1483-0 (sc)*
*ISBN: 979-8-8230-1482-3 (e)*

*Print information available on the last page.*

# PREFACE

As we look at Jesus and his 12 disciples, we will find that most of their journey of about three years was based on teachings that were not delivered in the parable but as clearly as possible to ease their understanding. These disciples grew in wisdom and knowledge of Jesus's new doctrines. With the outpouring of the Holy Spirit on the disciples, they were ready to preach the gospel without reluctance. They were zealous. Not only that, but they also didn't lose their faith. They pursue the way to the end despite tribulations, threats, and difficulties from so-called spiritual gurus. They continued carrying the vision and the work of our Lord Jesus Christ. They also formed disciples. I sincerely believe they could do great work because of the fundamental teachings that provided a solid foundation for their faith and spiritual growth.

I have noticed that many who give their life to Christ do not receive specific, straightforward, and "solid ground" teachings that can help them through their new life as Christians. Once they say, "Yes Lord, I accept you as my savior and shepherd," they are abandoned, left in struggles that will eventually lead them to backslide or be part of the group of Christians that say the church hurts them. That is sad, but the reality is there. Many newborn Christians are lukewarm, copying their lifestyle from the world instead of the bible and biblical principles. The problem is problematic. The devil is at war to bring those who left to his kingdom. Because of the worldly system and behavior in the churches, many people are losing faith and holy virtues.

I spent my entire childhood at church. I grew up at church. I saw many problems that newborn Christians go through to get to the top (if they do not backslide), which I also experienced. I have served God my entire life, building up experience through fellowship and mentoring new Christians to avoid traps.

It is precisely in this perspective that this book is coming. Maybe it won't solve all the problems that newborn Christians face, but it will help them stay focused, diligent, and responsible. Also, it will unveil every little trick the devil could use to quench brothers and sisters' faith.

As you read this book, you will discover simple yet essential tips to grow ideally in a good Christian atmosphere without significant struggles. This book is intended for folks making their first steps into the kingdom. It will not be a waste of time. You will also understand and can even teach others in your community some of these secrets. You will also understand why, where, and how you may have stumbled or made a mistake in your spiritual growth. I can guarantee you will not regret it. You will get a fire boost that will deal permanently with spiritual stagnation.

# FOREWORD

Shake the Nation (STN) is an annual gathering of leaders, professionals, and experts worldwide in Omaha, Nebraska. Martin Williams International has hosted the STN conference for thirty years at the Ambassador Worship Center. Leaders come to learn from other's experiences, discover themselves, develop their gifts and skills, and get deployed in the community to become world changers.

Eric Kouassi regularly attends the annual conference. I remember he was staring at me at one of the breakout sessions, and I knew he had a lot to tell me. I offered him to have a launch. This began a strong bond between the Kouassi family and the Williams. I am a Pastor and have seen many things believers struggle with. One of these problems is their inability to stay on track and focus and get the best out of their journey with the King of the Kingdom of Heaven.

As I read this book, I see it targets these believers. Suppose it offers a proven solution that can be taught at any church. He also stressed knowing yourself, your story, your past, and your future and having a spiritual covering. These few things stood out to me among many more subjects. As you might suspect, this book is an exciting and worthwhile read, and I highly recommend it.

Pastor Eric Kouassi is the kind of person you would want in the foxhole with you when everything breaks loose. You can count on him to coach and groom you to become a better version of yourself.

# ACKNOWLEDGMENT

I want to thank many people for helping me with this project.

First, my best friend for life, Desiree N. Zegbe, constantly pushes and encourages me to work and kill procrastination from my daily habits. She is a genuine support, always present in the good and the bad. I am forever grateful.

Second, my mother. She has always inspired me. She is more than a woman. She is a hard-working woman and always ready to fight for us. She never settles for less, always striving to offer my brothers and sister great joy and happiness to me.

Third, my congregation, every church member of the Overcomers Ministry Church of Omaha, spiritual sons and daughters. They give me a reason to stand in the gap for them. What a wonderful people of God. They always pray for me so God can use me in another dimension.

My old man (Mon Vieux père) Apostle Guy Tanoh Joseph. He is a man of excellence and revelation to be recommended.

Special thank you and acknowledgment to my kingdom family, Dr. Martin and Lynnell Williams. I thank this family for challenging me and teaching me to think profoundly and follow my dream while building a great kingdom family.

I also want to thank my brother, Pastor Olivier D. Sarr, who has so much knowledge of strategic success. As well as my sister, Prophetess Stephanie Abaka, and every man of God I have ever met who prayed and mentored me.

God bless you.

# TABLE OF CONTENTS

- Section 1: What is your former state?
- Section 2: What has the Lord done for you to be where you are today?
- Section 3: What and who are you today?
- Section 4: Always know where you are going in life and with God
- Section 5: Always carry your testimony
- Section 6: Try not to go back to your same old habits

- Section 1: Improve your relationship with God
- Section 2: Improve your life of consecration
- Section 3: Improve your prayer life
- Section 4: Improve your service to God at church and daily
- Section 5: Improve your relationship with other believers
- Section 6: Remove mediocrity and negligence from your habits

- Section 1: Define spiritual gauge
- Section 2: Know when you are at the lowest point of your spiritual life

# INTRODUCTION

## Who is God ~ Accepting Jesus Christ

Everything on Earth has a beginning, a date of birth, and a starting point. Everything God created or birthed has a beginning. Also, everything that has a beginning must end someday. Every being lives for a period, whether long or short. Only God breaks this principle. He is the Alpha and Omega, meaning "the beginning and the end." He starts everything and ends everything. Every rational person should recognize and confess this fact.

As the Bible says:

*He is the image of the invisible God, the firstborn over all creation. 16 For by Him all things were created that are in heaven and that are on Earth, visible and invisible, whether thrones or dominions or principalities or powers. All things were created through Him and for Him. 17 And He is before all things, and in Him all things consist. 18 And He is the head of the body, the church, who is the beginning, the firstborn from the dead, that in all things He may have the preeminence."* — *Colossians 1:15-18*

We understand in these verses that Jesus is at the center of everything. He is the head and unavoidable element of Christianity, our walk of faith. Yes, the name of Jesus is greater and more powerful than we can imagine. Can you imagine someone who is the physical representative of a God never seen but heard? Can you imagine someone being the sole basis of all creation and creatures? Jesus Christ is the center of the universe. He is the first to defy death, overcome death, defeat death, knowing that death is an exam that no one has ever failed. As we meditate on the Old Testament, the Holy Spirit can reveal to our spirit that almost every story, image, and character points to Jesus Christ. (We shall return to a study on Christ's centrality.) What a blessing.

God is God. God is holy. He is not holy once. He is three times holy.

*And one cried to another and said: Holy, holy, holy is the Lord of hosts; The whole Earth is full of His glory! — Isaiah 6:3*

God is good. God is beauty. God is perfect. God is love. God is loving-kindness; God is merciful. God is great and glorious.

*For You, Lord, are good, and ready to forgive, and abundant in mercy to all those who call upon You. — Psalms 86:5*

*The Lord is good to all, And His tender mercies are over all His works. — Psalms 145:60*

Beside him, there is no other God.

*I am the Lord, and there is no other. There is no God besides Me. I will gird you, though you have not known Me. — Isaiah 45:5*

Despite his holiness, he loves the sinner and doesn't desire death. God wants everyone to repent and come back to him. Only demons do not partake in the redemptive power of God. God is too holy. His holiness makes us holy, but he can't come to Earth in a glorious form; otherwise, the world could disappear. Imagine the effect of the atomic bomb released on Hiroshima and Nagasaki to the infinite power. Remember that God doesn't want any sinner to perish but to have salvation. As the Bible says:

*The Lord is not slack concerning His promise, as some count slackness, but is longsuffering toward us, not willing that any should perish but that all should come to repentance. — 2 Peter 3:9*

Yes, believe it or not, God wants all of us to be saved and part of his everlasting kingdom of heaven family.

Seeing humanity dominated by sin, evil actions, perversion, murder, stealing, prostitution, and wickedness, God's ultimate plan to save humankind is through the death of his son Jesus Christ at the cross.

*For God so loved the world that He gave His only begotten Son, that whoever believes in Him should not perish but have everlasting life. — John 3:16*

So, through his blood shed on the cross, we can receive forgiveness of sin and a restoration of a new covenant with God. We can be co-heir with Jesus of God, have dominion over Satan, and regain power over sin and the prince of this world.

*In Him, we have redemption through His blood, the forgiveness of sins, according to the riches of His grace. — Ephesians 1:7*

~~~**Wow, praise the Lord almighty God for this grace**~~~~

You receive salvation by accepting Jesus in your life and confessing your sins. Not only that, but you receive the power to become children of God.

*Repent therefore and be converted, that your sins may be blotted out, so that times of refreshing may come from the presence of the Lord. — Acts 3:19*

*But as many as received Him, to them He gave the right to become children of God, to those who believe in His name. — John 1:12*

Once a person repents and confesses his sin, meaning turning away from sin and iniquity, they perform a 180-degree complete turnaround. If it is well done, and they accept Jesus Christ as their savior, salvation just entered their life.

The Baptism of Water and the Spirit should follow next. After Baptism, there must be the manifestation of the gifts of the Spirit, mainly the gift of speaking in tongues. This is a powerful gift to help the newborn's first steps into the kingdom. It develops a prayer life by speaking the mysteries of God and filling our spiritual life with the fire of God. Contrary to what other preachers say, I would recommend every Christian to pray in tongues everywhere. There is no limit or specific place to speak in tongues. It is a gift of the Spirit and cannot be quenched or restrained. One must be free to exercise it as much as they want to. I will call it a free-will gift. It doesn't have to be translated, which implies the need for the gift of interpretation of tongues. We will come back to the gift of speaking in tongues.

Here is a small sketch that depicts the above explanation:

**Confession of sins and iniquity leads to repentance from sins. Forgiveness of sins leads to baptism of water and of the Holy Spirit. These will lead to manifesting the gifts of the Spirit and serving God. Everything is connected, and one thing leads to another.**

*I say to you that, likewise there will be more joy in heaven over one sinner who repents than over ninety-nine just persons who need no repentance. — Luke 15:7*

~~~ AMEN ~~~

# CHAPTER 1

# DO YOU KNOW WHERE YOU COME FROM?

*Listen to Me, you who follow after righteousness, you who seek the Lord: Look to the rock from which you were hewn, and to the hole of the pit from which you were dug.* — *Isaiah 51:1*

## Your Origin

Everything has an origin. Everything has a beginning, as we stated above. Your origin is where you come from. Where do you come from? I ask this question from the kingdom perspective, pointing to your source, God. Because you came out of God. However, I am also talking about what you used to be, your genetic origin, where your forefathers are from, your family's tree roots, and where everything about you and your family started.

The Oxford English Dictionary defines "origin" as the point or place where something begins, commences, starts, arises, or is derived.

In Africa, whenever you go out, and you find yourself in the middle of the drama, or you come across an older person who wants to know about your origin, they will ask very simple questions but very deep: "What is your name? What is your father's name? Which house are you from?

1

The answers to these questions reveal the name of the family, the story behind that family, their identity, and, of course, their origin.

Dear friends, know that your origin matters a lot in your spiritual life. If you ignore your origin and family history, seeking the truth and questioning your relatives is important.

*For inquire, I pray thee, of the former age, and prepare thyself to the search of their fathers. For we are but of yesterday, and know nothing, because our days upon earth are a shadow. — Job 8:8-9*

~~~~ **Your story and destiny are hidden in the name you carry**~~~~

Notice there is a difference between your first name and your last name. Your first name is the name you go by every day, that which everyone knows you by. But your last name is the name you usually inherit from your parents, your origin. Some people even call it their "family name."

I often see a program on television where people try to locate or determine their origin. They want to know whether their ancestors were Irish, Caucasian, or African. They are trying to find out where their ancestors are from so, they can know who they are and their true culture (because they live in a civilization with many mixed cultures).

There is something that defines every family. It could be a sickness (cancer, down syndrome, depression), stress, unbelief, religion, atheism, a character trait (anger, shyness, a running mouth, promiscuity), a blessing (gifts, academic success, prosperity), or even a generational curse (alcoholism, sudden death, miscarriage, stealing, shortcoming, failure), any problem. That issue, blessing, curse, or sickness is transmitted and distributed to each family member — boys and or girls — by the power of the blood. No one is exempt. Many families suffer from it (we will discuss generational curses and blessings in a future edition).

**Knowing your family history and origin will help you know where you come from, where you are going, and most importantly, "the spiritual warfare, spiritual battles, strongholds, strongmen, and demons that**

can cause hindrances in your Christian journey. That knowledge will let you experience a blessed and prosperous life.

## Your Former State

Everyone, without exception, comes to Christ in such a state that only God can turn or change their life around. The Bible is full of examples.

Your former state is the state in which you came to Christ with, the pain you carried to church, the sickness you were healed from, the brokenness you were delivered from, the yoke that was broken from your neck, the spirits that possessed and haunted your life, the demons you were dealing with, the unhappiness you were experiencing before entering into the house of God, the tribulation, adversity, rejection, confusion, depression, trial and mighty difficulties you were undergoing. These were the reasons that made you seek deliverance, a solution, and an answer from God. Your former state is why you were drawn to Christ Jesus and decided to make your first steps in the kingdom of heaven.

Here is a story in the gospel of Saint Luke depicting the above illustration.

*11 Soon afterward, he went to a town called Nain. His disciples and a great crowd went with him. 12 As he drew near the town gate, behold, a man who had died was being carried out, the only son of his mother. She was a widow, and a considerable crowd from the town was with her. 13 And when the Lord saw her, he had compassion and said to her, "Do not weep." 14 Then he came up and touched the bier, and the bearers stood still. And he said, "Young man, I say to you, arise." 15 And the dead man sat up and began to speak, and Jesus gave him to his mother. 16 Fear seized them all, and they glorified God, saying, "A great prophet has arisen among us!" and "God has visited his people!" 17 And this report about him spread through the whole of Judea and all the surrounding country. — Luke 7:11-17*

This is the story of a widow who lost her only son. The Spirit of death was all over her, and death had taken away the most important people of her life.

3

It is almost certain that she does not have too long to live. Death is in her house, in her bloodline. It is in the midst of all this chaos that she met Jesus or the kingdom. He resolves her problems, gives her deliverance, and comforts her. I am sure she believed and accepted Jesus as savior that very day. She made her first step into the kingdom of heaven. Let me remind you that her former state was dealing with the Spirit of death. When she met Jesus, everything changed.

### ~~~Never forget your former state ~~~

Your former state is your genesis and origin before you take your first step into this new life. You must never forget it. Always have it in your mind. I am not saying always to remember your pain and cry and mourn. It is the source of your testimony. Be cautious with it. Always remind yourself how you were, where you were, and the condition the Lord rescued you from by his mighty hand. You become automatically grateful and thankful for what the Lord has done for you by always reminding yourself about your former state. You must make up your mind not to return to how you used to be. It is a source of joy and celebration, not sadness.

**~~~ When you are in Christ, your past should not be shameful but a source of joy as you experience transformation. AMEN! ~~~**

## My Testimony

I came to Christ broken, sick, and suffering the fury of witches in my family. I felt death around me. My nights were very troubled with nightmares. I was sick to the point of hallucinating. I heard and saw things that made me run out of the house, crying for help. Many times, neighbors had to call my mother from work. I wanted to die. In my mind, it was logical. I loved to see funerals and caskets. At school, I would draw tombs with such precision and beauty. The Spirit of death was haunting my soul. I remember asking the pharmacist for medicine that would cause death. The pharmacist said, "No, we do not sell that type of medicine." I was doing this because I was mad at my parents and life. I could not do anything to change the situation. My only option was to kill myself or wish for death.

It is important to note that when the Spirit of death is after you, living no longer matters to you. You want to die. You are not conscious of the dangerous game you are playing. Demons influence your normal thinking patterns, actions, reactions, and character. You know a person is possessed by a certain type of demon through what they do. For instance, a demon of alcoholism would make someone an alcoholic and a demon of prostitution would make a woman give herself to a man for money. A demon of theft would make someone steal, and so on. Let us not be ignorant of the devices of the enemies.

All these situations happened to me even though I grew up in a Christian home. My mother was a prayer warrior, and my sister was a believer. But only God knows how many people grew up in Christian homes without personal experience or encounters with God. Demons manipulate them. May the Lord God Almighty help us.

The Bible contains examples of people coming to Jesus Christ sick, broken, and devastated. Here is another example.

*And a certain man was there, who had an infirmity of thirty and eight years. When Jesus saw him lie and knew that he had been now a long time in that case, he saith unto him, wilt thou be made whole? — John 5:5*

This poor man was sick and paralyzed for 38 years. Can you imagine how hopeless and desperate he was? That was his former condition, his former state. Thirty-eight years of sickness is a very long time, almost a lifetime.

As you read this book, any issue is quenched and pulled out of your life in the name of Jesus Christ, our everlasting Father.

*9 And he said to his people, "Look, the people of the children of Israel are more and mightier than we; 10 come, let us deal shrewdly with them, lest they multiply, …" 11 Therefore they set taskmasters over them to afflict them with their burdens. And they built for Pharaoh supply cities, Pithom and Raamses. 12 But the more they afflicted them, the more they multiplied and grew. And they were in dread of the children of Israel. 13 So the Egyptians made the children of Israel serve with rigor. 14 And they made their lives bitter with hard bondage—in mortar, in brick, and in all manner of service in the field. All their service in which they made them serve was with rigor. — Exodus 1:9-15*

The people of Israel — the people of God — were under severe bondage, in total slavery, for more than 400 years before being delivered from Egypt. Their former condition was slavery, serving an evil master without a salary.

If you are under any slavery as you read this book, may the mighty power of God touch you and set you free in the name of Jesus Christ.

*Then Saul, still breathing threats and murder against the disciples of the Lord, went to the high priest 2 and asked letters from him to the synagogues of Damascus, so that if he found any who were of the wayway, whether men or women, he might bring them bound to Jerusalem. 3 As he journeyed he came near Damascus, and suddenly a light shone around him from heaven. 4 Then he fell to the ground, and heard a voice saying to him, "Saul, Saul, why are you persecuting Me?" 5 And he said, "Who are You, Lord?" — Acts 9:1-5*

Apostle Paul was a murderer, anointed by the devil to attack Christians and spread his tradition, Judaism. His former state had multiple facets, like many people: hatred, murder, bloodthirstiness, arrogance, rebellion against God, anti-Christ, and so on.

May the Lord visit any family member who hates, threatens, and attacks you because you gave your life to Christ, pray in tongues, fast regularly, and attend church every Sunday.

*Now it happened, the day after, that He went into a city called Nain, and many of His disciples went with Him, and a large crowd. 12 And when He came near the gate of the city, behold, a dead man was being carried out, the only son of his mother; and she was a widow. And a large crowd from the city was with her. — Luke 7:11-12*

Back to our first example:

This woman was a widow. She met Jesus, still grieving the loss of her husband. Now, she had lost her only son. Even the presence of the crown at that moment would not comfort her or replace what she had lost. Do you know that no one can restore what you have lost in your life except Jesus? (He can restore peace, love, spiritual hunger, stability, health, and wealth.) Her state before the resurrection of her son was emotional pain, grief, brokenness, and emptiness, with the Spirit of death devastating her house.

In the name of Jesus, as you hold this book in your hands, may the Holy Spirit fill every emptiness in your soul. May he remove any pain, grief, and brokenness you are going through now. I rebuke every Spirit of death in the name of Jesus.

Always remember where you come from. It will help you in your future journey. Never delete your former state from your memory. It might make you careless and fall back into your old self and life. Be conscious of where you come from. And declare it, say it to yourself: "I shall never go back to the old me." You will save your life in this way.

Remember, according to the Bible, when a demon leaves one's life, it always comes back to check if their life is clean, well-organized, and Holy Spirit-filled. Otherwise, they get seven more powerful demons to come and possess the body. His later condition becomes worse than his former.

*When an unclean spirit goes out of a man, he goes through dry places, seeking rest, and finds none. 44 Then he says, "I will return to my house from which I came." And when he comes, he finds it empty, swept, and put in order. 45 Then he goes and takes with him seven other spirits more wicked than himself, and they enter and dwell there; and the last state of that man is worse than the first. So, shall it also be with this wicked generation. — Matthew 12:43-45*

We ought to keep that responsibility and declare:

~~~ **"I will never go back"** ~~~

**What did the Lord do for you to be where you are today?**

There is a big difference between your *former state coming to Christ* and *what the Lord has done for you.* As explained above, your former state is the problem, issue, sickness, and demons you carried into becoming a Christian. Now, we define "What the Lord has done for you" as the transforming miracles the power of the Holy Ghost subjected to you.

You cannot come to Christ and remain as you are. The Lord, our miracle worker, must and must do something to demonstrate his lordship on earth and every human being. That is the healing power of God mentioned in the book of Isaiah.

*The Spirit of the Lord God is upon me, Because the Lord has anointed me to preach good tidings to the poor; He has sent me to heal the brokenhearted, to proclaim liberty to the captives, and the opening of the prison to those who are bound; 2 to proclaim the acceptable year of the Lord, and the day of vengeance of our God; to comfort all who mourn, 3 to console those who mourn in Zion, to give them beauty for ashes, the oil of joy for mourning, the garment of praise for the Spirit of heaviness; that they may be called trees of righteousness, the planting of the Lord, that He may be glorified. — Isaiah 61:1-3*

Always recognize what the Lord has done for you. After recognizing what you used to be, we can never measure the Lord's good work in our lives. Every day, every time, God's loving kindness, compassion, and grace are poured out upon us. Healing miracles, deliverances, breakthroughs, divine protection, and much more are our daily bread. You can never stop counting everything the Lord does. Even when we see it, we must acknowledge that we didn't make it on our own. We must acknowledge that a supernatural being, the most high Jehovah, was working behind the scenes for our good. God will not explain or list every little thing he did for us. But if we have the Holy Spirit, the Spirit that reveals God's mind, we will know in our heart that his hand was, is, and shall always be upon us. We should list everything imaginable that we got from God. Those are gifts from above.

**~~~ List everything the Lord has done for you, from before
you were saved, during and after conversion~~~**

Sometimes we take everything for granted. Ungratefulness is our second nature. Can we pay for the air we breathe? Since the air owner is called El-Elohim, we would all be in debt. Can you pay your life bill? Since he owns the Free Life-Giving Company, we must fill our days with less complaints and more thanksgiving, prayers, and songs. Just like David said:

*Make a joyful shout to the Lord, all you land! 2 Serve the Lord with gladness; Come before His presence with singing. 3 Know that the Lord, He is God; It is He who has made us, and not we ourselves; We are His people and the sheep of His pasture. 4 Enter into His gates with thanksgiving, And into His courts with praise. Be thankful to Him, and bless His name. 5 For the Lord is good; His mercy is everlasting, And His truth endures to all generations.* — *Psalms 100:1-5*

When tribulations and trials come, we instantly forget everything God did for us. We forget everything God has done for us, making us think God is evil; however, God is not and can never be evil.

**~Every day, in good times and bad, repeat
it to yourself: God is good~~**

At my conversion, I had a sickness called sinusitis. That illness causes a bad smell that comes out of the nose. The cavities around the nasal passages become inflamed due to bacteria in the mucus and sinuses. At times, it hurts with a burning sensation. The burning sensation increased when I tried to fast. This bad-smelling mucus would drop in my mouth, and that caused pain in my stomach. People noticed that bad smell as they approached me. It was embarrassing and shameful at the same time.

**~~~I pray in the name of Jesus that every situation causing you
discomfort be removed in the name of Jesus Christ. ~~~**

One day, as I was sleeping, I had a dream. in my dream, I saw an angel telling me to blow my nose. As I was doing so, I saw a huge maggot coming out of my nose. I woke up dismayed and surprised, wondering what kind of dream this was.

Later, it came into my mind to blow my nose, and to my surprise, there was no sense of sinusitis, no pressure on the back of my head, and no bad smell around me. To this day, I have not experienced that shameful sickness again. Glory be to God!

### ~~~ May this testimony be your portion ~~~~

The Bible contains stories of people who experienced total change because of what Adonai has done for them.

*So, it came to pass in the process of time that Hannah conceived and bore a son- and called his name Samuel, saying, "Because I have asked for him from the Lord." — 1 Samuel 1:20* The Lord visited Hannah, and she went from barrenness to pregnant

*Then Nebuchadnezzar went near the mouth of the burning fiery furnace and spoke, saying, "Shadrach, Meshach, and Abed-Nego, servants of the Most High God, come out, and come here." Then Shadrach, Meshach, and Abed-Nego came from the midst of the fire. — Daniel 3:26*

The Lord delivered Daniel and his companion from the fiery furnace, provoking praise all over Babylon because they trusted their God.

*So, he sent and brought him in. Now he was ruddy, with bright eyes, and good-looking. And the Lord said, "Arise, anoint him; for this is the one!" — 1 Samuel 16:12*

The Lord made David a king over Israel. He removed him from behind the sheep to Zion. He anointed him king, a man according to God's heart.

### ~~~May the Lord take you from slavery to dominion. ~~~

Through God, we will do valiantly, for *it is* He *who* shall tread down our enemies. AMEN!

## What and who are you today?

Who are you today? From when you left your former life and became Christian, you can't tell me that nothing changed in you, your soul, your spirit, your body, your mind, your finances, or your status.

What is your status compared to your past?

- Were you jobless, and did the Lord gave you a job?
- Were you single, and did the Lord gave you a husband or a wife?
- Did you have any promotion at work since you got saved?
- Were you financially bankrupted, but the Lord changed it so that today you have financial freedom?
- Were you homeless, but the Lord gave you a house, a place to stay?

Look at you today. See the *GLORY* of God over you. Look how God crowned you with *GLORY* and *POWER*.

The Bible says:

*Behold, I give unto you power to tread on serpents and scorpions, and over all the power of the enemy: and nothing shall by any means hurt you.* — *Luke 10:19*

*For You have made him a little lower than the angels, and You have crowned him with glory and honor.* — *Psalms 8:5*

How do you see yourself today? Do you look down on yourself, or do you have low self-esteem? How do you see yourself after your conversion, after your first step in the kingdom of God? There must be a great change in how you perceive yourself now that you are born again.

Do you know who you are? Do you know that you are the child of the most high God? Do you know that as soon as you say yes, Lord, I accept you, His Spirit abides in you?

As the Bible says:

*For you are all sons of God through faith in Christ Jesus.* — *Galatians 3:26*

*For all who are being led by the Spirit of God, these are sons of God.* — *Roman 8:14*

Do you know that you are forgiven for *any* sin (even the worst ones) you have committed by the precious and powerful blood of the lamb?

*If we confess our sins, He is faithful and righteous to forgive us our sins and to cleanse us from all unrighteousness.* — *1 John 1:9*

Do you know Satan has nothing against you, and he can't kill you? Because you are hidden under the shadow of the Highest. Do you know that you are untouchable, unkillable, unstoppable, unbreakable? Do you know that you can cast demons out?

*Jesus summoned His twelve disciples and gave them authority over unclean spirits, to cast them out, and to heal every kind of disease and every kind of sickness.* — *Matthew 10:1*

*Heal the sick, raise the dead, cleanse the lepers, cast out demons. Freely you received, freely give.* — *Matthew 10:8*

Do you know that you are a spiritual being? Because you are a spiritual being, you can now hear and understand the voice of God. Therefore, you should not be led by flesh.

*The wind blows where it wishes, and you hear the sound of it, but cannot tell where it comes from and where it goes. So is everyone who is born of the Spirit.* — *John 3:8*

Do you know that you are a co-heir with Jesus Christ? It means that we are legally entitled to every blessing and grace of God. Moreover, we share these heavenly favors with Jesus. Do you understand that you are blessed?

*And if children, then heirs—heirs of God and joint heirs with Christ, if indeed we suffer with Him, that we may also be glorified together.* — Romans 8:17

Do you know that you are part of a new covenant with God through the blood of Jesus?

Do you know that you are partaker of the blessing of Abraham? Do you know that you are blessed, and no one can curse you when you become a Christian? Do you understand that the precious blood of Jesus has redeemed you? Do you know that you can claim every blessing and promise in the Bible?

*In Him, we have redemption through His blood, the forgiveness of our trespasses, according to the riches of His grace.* — Ephesians 1:7

*Christ redeemed us from the curse of the law, having become a curse for us - for it is written, "CURSED IS EVERYONE WHO HANGS ON A TREE"* — Galatians 3:13

Do you know that even demons fear you? They can attack or intimidate you but cannot do you any harm. Do you know that you have authority over them? Do you know you can cast them out, destroy them, scatter them in the mighty name of Jesus?

Do you know your new identity in Christ? Do you know that if Christ is for you, no one can be against you?

*What, then, shall we say to these things? If God is for us, who can be against us?* — Romans 8:31

Do you know that angels, the hosts of heaven, are at your service? God sent them to minister to you and provide for all your needs. Yes, angels are your helpers in every task related to your destiny and mission if you comply and follow God's plan.

*Then the devil left Him, and behold, angels came and ministered to Him.* — Matthew 4:11

*But the prince of the kingdom of Persia was withstanding me for 21 days; then behold, Michael, one of the chief princes, came to help me, for I had been left there with the kings of Persia. — Daniel 10:3*

You must know, understand, recognize, and master your new position in Christ Jesus. You must know the privileges associated with your conversion. When you know these spiritual truths, your faith is rooted deep in Christ, giving you a boldness that will be essential for the rest of the journey.

If you were to be asked, "Who are you today?" You must be able to provide such an accurate answer that it would make the person listening to you speechless and dismayed. Yes, I am talking about your identity in the kingdom. Through your answer, people will discern whether you became a Christian out of fashion or through conviction.

Unfortunately, some Christians don't know who and what they are in Christ. It is not too late to go back and restudy all the questions above so you can draw an image of your new nature.

May the truth no longer be hidden from us in Jesus' name.

In the kingdom, what is ignored is dangerous. It is a potentially opened door that the devil can use to destroy you. My people perish because of a lack of knowledge.

~~~ **The most important thing a Christian should know is their identity in Christ. Always carry your spiritual ID card** ~~

**Always know where you are going in life and with God.**

Connected to your origin and background, a very important question arises: "Where are you going in your life with God?" This is a very important interrogation addressed to each believer as a banner to capture their attention.

As we wander through the scriptures, we understand that God rarely uses anyone who does not get busy. Our master, Jesus Christ, called his disciples out of their busy schedules and then told them what they would do next. He was literally saying that you were doing that, but from now on, you will be doing this.

For example, we can recall the following:

- Elisha was plowing with 12 yokes of oxen before receiving Elijah's mantle to become a prophet of the Lord after him. *(1 Kings 19:15-20)*

*15 Then the Lord said to him: "Go, return on your way to the Wilderness of Damascus; and when you arrive, anoint Hazael as king over Syria. 16 Also, you shall anoint Jehu, the son of Nimshi as king over Israel. And Elisha, the son of Shaphat of Abel Meholah, you shall anoint as prophet in your place. 17 It shall be that whoever escapes the sword of Hazael, Jehu will kill; and whoever escapes the sword of Jehu, Elisha will kill. 18 Yet I have reserved 7000 in Israel, all whose knees have not bowed to Baal, and every mouth that has not kissed him." 19 So he departed from there, and found Elisha the son of Shaphat, who was plowing with 12 yoke of oxen before him, and he was with the 12th. Then Elijah passed by him and threw his mantle on him. 20 And he left the oxen and ran after Elijah, and said, "Please let me kiss my father and my mother, and then I will follow you."*

*And he said to him, "Go back again, for what have I done to you?"* — *1 Kings 19:15-20*

- Moses was tending the sheep of his father-in-law when the Lord called from the burning bush. *(Exodus 3:1-17)*

*1 Now Moses was tending the flock of Jethro, his father-in-law, the priest of Midian. And he led the flock to the back of the desert, and came to Horeb, the mountain of God. 2 And the Angel of the Lord appeared to him in a flame of fire from the midst of a bush. So, he looked, and behold, the bush was burning with fire, but the bush was not consumed. 3 Then Moses said, "I will now turn aside and see this great sight, why the bush does not burn."*

*4 So when the Lord saw that he turned aside to look, God called to him from the midst of the bush and said, "Moses, Moses!"*

*And he said, "Here I am."*

*5 Then He said, "Do not draw near this place. Take your sandals off your feet, for the place where you stand is holy ground." 6 Moreover He said, "I am the God of your father—the God of Abraham, the God of Isaac, and the God of Jacob." And Moses hid his face, for he was afraid to look upon God.*

*7 And the Lord said: "I have surely seen the oppression of My people who are in Egypt, and have heard their cry because of their taskmasters, for I know their sorrows. 8 So I have come down to deliver them out of the hand of the Egyptians, and to bring them up from that land to a good and large land, to a land flowing with milk and honey, to the place of the Canaanites and the Hittites and the Amorites and the Perizzites and the Hivites and the Jebusites. 9 Now therefore, behold, the cry of the children of Israel has come to Me, and I have also seen the oppression with which the Egyptians oppress them. 10 Come now, therefore, and I will send you to Pharaoh that you may bring My people, the children of Israel, out of Egypt. — Exodus 3:1-10*

- Jesus called Peter, Andrew, James, and John. They went from fishermen to fishers of men.

*18 And Jesus, walking by the Sea of Galilee, saw two brothers, Simon called Peter, and Andrew his brother, casting a net into the sea; for they were fishermen. 19 Then He said to them, "Follow Me, and I will make you fishers of men." 20 They immediately left their nets and followed Him. 21 Going on from there, He saw two other brothers, James, the son of Zebedee, and John, his brother, in the boat with Zebedee, their Father, mending their nets. He called them 22, and immediately they left the boat and their Father and followed Him. — Matthew 4:18-22*

When you become Christian, the Lord God changes your story. He changes your life. But that doesn't mean you should stay at the same level and not progress spiritually and professionally.

I always tell newborn Christians that they should have goals and visions when stepping into the kingdom of heaven. Before the kingdom, you were all alone, running your life and heading in any direction you wanted to. But now, Jesus is in the boat, and Jesus is in your life. He is the captain running the boat, your life.

Let's take the example of someone who used to work for a small company, making a small amount of money, with many problems, such as sickness, rejection, and depression. When he encountered Christ Jesus, his life changed. He was healed, and he had peace. He no longer goes to the hospital. All this is good. But it shouldn't stop there. There is more. That person must fulfill his destiny and set goals and visions. Just because you are a Christian who speaks in tongues and holds a bible doesn't mean you shouldn't go to school, get a higher education, read books, and cultivate yourself. Aiming for a higher position or promotion at work, opening, or owning businesses is not against the culture of the kingdom of heaven. Christians should be excellent, pursuing success once they find God's kingdom and righteousness.

**~~~ If you know where you are going, you will always be happy. People who don't know where they are going are always confused. ~~~**

Your story is different from other people's; therefore, don't race with anyone. Don't compete with anyone. Just be yourself and focus on becoming greater than you are today or what you used to be. You must decide clearly in your heart that with Jesus, you will live a better life. Never let confusion take over. If you feel confused about where you are going in life and with God, take a time of fasting and prayer. Ask God, what did you call me for? What position do you want me to be in? What is my mission on Earth? Pray, Jesus, just as you called the 12 disciples and told them what they would do (from fishermen to fisher of men); please, Lord, tell me, show me what you called me for. Better yet, find a mentor to help you figure that out.

*Jesus said to him, "I am the way, the truth, and the life. No one comes to the Father except through Me." — John 14:6*

*I will instruct you and teach you in the way you should go; I will guide you with My eye. — Psalms 32:8*

Yes, He is the way, so He will show you the way when you are confused. Once you receive an answer, stick it in your mind, make it part of your DNA, work on it, press on it, develop your gifts and talents, and *be focused*. You will be blessed, I promise you.

The very next thing I suggest a new Christian to do is to look for his purpose. Where do you want to go in your new experience with Christ Jesus? What are you existing for? What are you living for? What are you breathing for?

Everything that exists and ever existed is for a purpose. Whatever God created has a purpose in it. Your purpose is the reason you live. If someone tells me they do not know their purpose, they are telling me they do not know why they are on Earth. An airplane is created to fly in the air, and a car exists to drive on the road from point A to point Z. Everything exists for a reason. Nothing God created is waste or meaningless. God created you for something. It would be best if you found it.

Anything that misses its purpose is easily broken. Anything that misses its purpose is perverted. If you know how God works, you will understand that you are not an accident. If you are not an accident, you are not a mistake. If your mother got pregnant while playing, she made a mistake, but you are not a mistake. You are not a stranger to nature.

> *~~~ It is not luck, fate, chance, or coincidence that you are breathing right now ~~~*

God deliberately chose your race, color, skin, hair, mother, Father, gender, citizenship, potential, and purpose. Everything fits you the way you should be. God determined the uniqueness of your talents and your personality.

> *~~ Without God, life has no purpose, and without purpose, life has no meaning~*

FIRST STEPS IN THE KINGDOM:

*Without purpose, there is no hope.*

"The greatest tragedy is life without purpose; it is not death," according to Dr. Myles Munroe.

Brethren, always know where you are going with God. Know what you are born to do. If not, pray and ask God to show you the way.

**Always carry your testimony.**

Go everywhere with your testimony. Please do not be ashamed of it. It tells everyone who sees you where you are coming from and the cause of your praise and worship of God.

**~~~If you don't know where you are going, at least know where God rescued you from~~~**

*Jesus said to him, "Rise, take up your bed and walk." 9 And immediately, the man was made well, took up his bed, and walked. — John 5:8-9*

In the story of the man healed at the pool of Bethesda, Jesus walked up to him and said: "Rise, take up your bed and walk." The story is full of revelation from the first to the last. However, let us focus on what we are interested in. Why would Jesus tell the man to take his bed and walk? Why couldn't Jesus say, "Stand up and walk?" Why is it that Jesus had to add, "Take up your bed" specifically? What does the bed represent? As I interrogate the Holy Spirit, he replies: The man was sick. He had lain on the bed for 38 years of suffering. He would always be on that bed if he were sick. The bed was evidence of his former condition after his healing. So, everywhere he goes, people will recognize him through the bed. Also, anytime he sees his bed, he will recall the 38 years of pain and agony Jesus rescued him from. You have no idea how many lives may be transformed by hearing your story. Tell people what Jesus did for you. In the Bible, Jesus would forbid people to mention his name or urge them to tell nobody who he was after he healed them. However, the miracle was so marvelous that they would scream, shout, and tell everybody what Jesus did as soon as they left the scene. Do not hide your story. Write a book, make short videos, and share your testimony in some way to boost one's faith.

**~~~Just like the man at the pool of Bethesda, wear your testimony proudly with no regrets. ~~~**

**Stay away from your old ways.**

In the many years, I have served God, one of the most devastating, heartbreaking things I keep seeing is "backsliding Christians." These are those who return to their old habits and old self. If it pains me, how much more does it pain God, our Father, creator of the universe, who loves us to the point of giving his son at the cross to save us eternally?

Those Christians were not able to commit. They could not hide under the shadow of the most high God. They forgot where the Lord brought them from, or they didn't set goals and a vision of where they wanted to go with the Lord. They were not courageous or dedicated enough. They may have taken salvation for granted and were not careful enough to avoid the enemies' traps. Maybe their conversion was not total. No matter the cause of the fall, the enemy was able to pull them back and make them possibly leave the faith.

In the next chapters, we will develop tips to help brothers and sisters in the walk with the Lord so they will not backslide.

We should not ignore the devices of the enemies we are fighting against. Once you get loosened from his grip, he will do anything to bring you back or to kill you. Conversion is a big and joyful event, but your life with Christ differs. It is a lifetime journey, and Satan doesn't rejoice about your salvation.

**~~~ Be ready for war~~~**

To not go back to your former ways, be ready for war. Do everything it takes. This is why I always tell everyone to be focused. During Jesus' earthly ministry, he would give them very important recommendations to follow every time he healed someone to not return to their old life.

*When Jesus had lifted up himself, and saw none but the woman, he said unto her, woman, where are those thine accusers? Hath no man condemned thee? She said, No man, Lord. And Jesus said unto her, neither do I condemn thee: go and sin no more. — John 8:10- 11*

Jesus said, "Go and sin no more." Jesus was saying to the adulterous woman, change your life. I don't condemn you, so no one else does either. However, don't give yourself to sin anymore. Don't go there because it is your past life, lest you expose yourself to the devil.

*Afterward Jesus findeth him in the temple, and said unto him, Behold, thou art made whole: sin no more, lest a worse thing come unto thee. — John 5:14*

What Jesus told the man was clear and simple: Brother, you are truly free today; the sickness and paralysis are gone. Now, you ought to be *extremely* careful. Do not backslide.

**~~~Do whatever it takes not to backslide. Do whatever it takes to not return to your old self and deeds. In so doing, you will save your life and grow up in the Lord peacefully. ~~~~~**

**Important:**

Even if there comes a time when you fall back, do not deny God. Keep your faith. No one is perfect. You will fail many times as you grow before finally getting it right. If you keep your eyes on Jesus and the cross, you will always get back on your feet. As the Bible says:

*For a righteous man may fall seven times
And rise again,*

*But the wicked shall fall by calamity.* — *Proverbs 24:16*

The wicked are the ones who know that there is a God but deliberately decide to reject God. Do not reject or deny God, Jesus, or the Holy Spirit under any circumstances.

# CHAPTER 2

# ALWAYS SEEK IMPROVEMENT

In 2007, coming home from a long day at work, I found a notice at my door. It wasn't a notice of eviction but a notice from the leasing office telling us to move out of the apartment in three months because a series of remodeling and improvements would be conducted on the premises. These improvements required all tenants to move out. The complex looked old. The owner needed to upgrade everything (kitchen, living room, bedroom, bathroom). The project was about raising the standard of the complex to fit customers' needs. Even though the project was costly, it needed to be marketable in the challenging competition between other rental companies.

I currently own a Windows desktop computer. Occasionally, the computer will undergo a long process of updates involving security, speed, look, and design. All these updates are to meet customers' needs since everything in the world is changing.

These examples reflect how we should continuously seek improvement in our spiritual life. We must go from one level to the next level, improving our spiritual life to please God and ourselves. We must improve our spiritual life to detect the enemy and expose his plan.

As a new convert into the kingdom, you need to know that there are many improvements. Each type of improvement is very important. If you don't pay attention to all of them, it could be costly. Let's go into the list.

**Improve your relationship with God.**

You may ask: What is it to improve my relationship with the Lord, and how is it done? Well, to improve your relationship with God is the fact that a Christian develops a strong desire day by day to get their communion with God in a better state, if not nearly perfect. It is to be more serious about His ways and laws. It is to be more mindful of Him by making Him the centerpiece of your life. To improve your relationship with God is to get better at talking to Him and to hear Him whenever he talks.

It is done by first:

- knowing things are not all right between your God and you. My friends, when things are not right in your relationship with God, you will know it. You must know when the Spirit is not agreeing with what you are doing and saying.
- You must know what the Bible calls our *"first love."*

*Nevertheless, I have this against you, that you have left your first love* — *Revelation 2:4*

If there is a first love, there should be a second love. The question is, what should the first love look like? It is more about feelings than actions. It is to have God in your mind more often than anything else. It is to have God in your heart more than any earthly thing. It is basically to think, feel, and experience God.

- Lastly, treat him as if you are in love with a physical body (we shall come back to this)

As I watched a love story in a movie, I realized that couples that fall out or split apart for many reasons (infidelity, money, in-laws...) but are still in love tend to come back together by promising not to make the same mistake they made before. They acknowledge one another's faults and change their ways and behavior to not cause emotional wounds to each other again. In Christian jargon, this is referred to as "repentance." It means to return from sin and evil ways back to the Lord through the process of repentance.

*Repent therefore and be converted, that your sins may be blotted out, so that times of refreshing may come from the presence of the Lord. — Acts 3:19*

Often, because of our flesh, lust, and temptation, we fall short and jeopardize our relationship with the Lord. A bad relationship with the Lord is visible.

There are many consequences of a bad relationship with the Lord:

- No more inner peace and, therefore, no real joy.
- A guilty mind
- Shame and feelings of resentment toward oneself.
- Laziness and lack of commitment to spiritual activities.
- Lack of seriousness and discipline in spiritual matters.
- Running away from saints (isolation)
- Adopting worldly behavior
- Becoming less and less sensitive to the Holy Spirit.
- Becoming an easy target for the devil.

You may ask me, "Well, pastor, what does a good relationship with the Lord look like?" We know that just because a couple appears in public laughing and saying nice words to each other does not mean the union is healthy.

Just because a married woman posts how much she loves her partner on social media does not mean the relationship is stable.

**~~~A real and healthy relationship starts in a secret place at home, in the closet or behind the door ~~~**

- A good relationship with the Lord starts with respecting His personality.
- A good relationship with the Lord is when you talk regularly and honestly every day in secret, not only in public and on Sunday.

- A good relationship with the Lord is when you love Him in the good times and bad. It is called unconditional love.
- A good relationship with the Lord is when you love the Lord with all your soul, mind, heart, and strength.
- A healthy relationship with the Lord happens when the Holy Spirit fills you.
- A healthy relationship with the Lord is when you read, study, and meditate daily on His word.
- Having a good relationship with the people around you is also essential.
- You must love and care about your neighbor.
- It includes serving Him and consecrating yourself to Him.

**Improve your life of consecration.**

As you grow in the Lord, you will go through many steps, each very important. One of these steps is consecration. Many people neglect this important step, emphasizing the less important.

The Bible says:

*Pursue peace with all people and holiness, without which no one will see the Lord: looking carefully lest anyone fall short of the grace of God; lest any root of bitterness springing up cause trouble, and by this many become defiled. — Hebrews 12:14-15*

Holiness is what will make you approach and see God. God is holy; therefore, we must be holy. Holiness is an attribute of God, one of his many characteristics. It is the absolute cleaning and purity of God. There is no spot of sin or uncleanness in him.

Consecration is when one is set apart for God. Everything set apart for God is holy and consecrated. It is sacred. That which belongs to God must not be touched or used for any other purpose than for God. When something is consecrated to God or by God, it must have that attribute and characteristic of holiness. Any sin or iniquity must not stain this life of consecration and holiness.

*And you shall be holy to Me, for I the Lord am holy, and have separated you from the peoples, that you should be Mine.* — Leviticus 20:26

This is God speaking to the people of Israel. God gave a list of elements forbidden to touch and certain categories of animals to not eat. God gave them a law not to break. The consequences of breaking this law were disastrous.

Holiness is not something to take lightly.

Holiness is not one's self-declaration that I will be pure. No one can or has the power to declare themselves pure in his own eyes or by himself. Only God can declare you "holy" before His own eyes, enabling you to approach Him despite your imperfections. Therefore, holiness is a gift of God to every believer. That is why you are called saints, which is another way of calling you holy.

Now, consecration is another story. It is when, while already holy, you devote yourself to what pleases God by giving yourself mentally, emotionally, spiritually, and physically.

It is when you set yourself apart for God temporarily or for life.

But one question remains: How can we maintain a good life of consecration or improve it to have a long-lasting Christian life?

- Always know that you belong to God and nothing else.
- You are set apart for God only and no one else.
- Everything you do must be for the glory of God and no one else.
- Always give glory to God and no one else, even yourselves.
- Do not touch anything forbidden by God. It could be alcohol, cigarettes, any drug, cursing…
- A consecrated person must run away from sin by any means.
- Cultivate a habit of spending time in the presence of God.

**~~~ consecration helps maintain your anointing. It helps the anointing remain clean and pure ~~~**

Christians should day by day work on their consecration life so they may approach the throne of glory with joy and no shame. We should not have a guilty mind, and there shall not be anything of the devil in us.

*Let your garments always be white,*

*And let your head lack no oil.* — *Ecclesiastes 9:8*

**Improve your prayer life.**

Prayer is your platform to talk to God. It is a conduit between God and you through which angels go up and down. Prayer is your invitation to God to intervene in cases and situations. Your prayer life is proportional to your faith, time, and respect toward God. Prayer is a principle because every God must be prayed to, praised, worshipped, and served.

You can only access heavenly riches and blessings if you pray. You can never access God's glory unless you pray. Prayer moves the hands of God. From the time of Adam and Eve, God could not come on Earth and invade human daily affairs unless He was invited through prayer.

Prayer is as powerful as the most powerful bomb humans ever made. Just as you can reach someone via phone living on the other side of the world, you can pray for someone living 1,000 miles away. Words are powerful. Internal or external prayer (praying in your heart and praying out loud) is powerful.

Many stories in the Bible depict how lives were changed through the power of prayer. When people pray, God has no other option than to answer brutally and dangerously. Satan cannot stop your mouth from opening to talk to God. He cannot stop your prayers but discourage you from praying. He can make you believe that God doesn't answer prayers fast enough. There is power in your prayer.

Therefore, these simple arithmetic stands are proven:

$$\sim\sim\text{ \textbf{Prayer + Faith = Miracle} }\sim\sim$$

**Here are some examples in the Bible of people who prayed and changed lives:**

*Then they cried out to the Lord in their trouble,*

*And He saved them out of their distresses. — Psalms 107:19*

*And Jabez called on the God of Israel, saying, "Oh, that You would bless me indeed, and enlarge my territory, that Your hand would be with me, and that You would keep me from evil, that I may not cause pain!" So, God granted him what he requested. — 1 Chronicles 4:10*

*Confess your trespasses to one another, and pray for one another, that you may be healed. The effective, event prayer of a righteous man avails much. — James 5:16*

*And she was in bitterness of soul, and prayed to the Lord and wept in anguish. 11 Then she made a vow and said, "O Lord of hosts, if You will indeed look on the affliction of Your maidservant and remember me, and not forget Your maidservant, but will give Your maidservant a male child, then I will give him to the Lord all the days of his life, and no razor shall come upon his head."*

*12 And it happened, as she continued praying before the Lord, that Eli watched her mouth. 13 Now Hannah spoke in her heart; only her lips moved, but her voice was not heard. Therefore, Eli thought she was drunk. — 1 Samuel 1:10-13*

*So Abraham prayed to God; and God healed Abimelech, his wife, and his female servants. Then, they bore children. — Genesis 20:17*

*Pray without ceasing. — 1 Thessalonians 5:17*

If the prayer of Jabez had been timed, it would not have lasted one minute. But God listened to him and granted him his request. Sometimes, the length of prayer does not matter. Repeating and multiplying nonsense words to God will not force God to answer your prayer. However, faith gives energy and power to your prayer. Also, as you grow spiritually, you will observe that God will draw you to pray more. God will prompt you to pray longer, at least one hour of prayer a day.

### ~~~ *Prayer is the activity of spiritual people* ~~~

*Then He came to the disciples and found them sleeping, and said to Peter, "What! Could you not watch with Me one hour? **41** Watch and pray, lest you enter into temptation. The Spirit indeed is willing, but the flesh is weak." —* *Matthew 26:40-41*

In these verses, we comprehend through what Jesus says that *prayer is a must.* We must be self-disciplined to pray. If you used to pray for five minutes, that is okay, but that must increase to 30 minutes, then one hour, and so on. The longer you pray, the easier it becomes to tap into the spiritual realm and receive revelations.

I asked an elder in the ministry one day how the anointing I saw on him flowed so easily, allowing his ministry to expand so that he had to add more seats to welcome the inflow of new members. He replied, "I set time aside to pray five to eight hours daily. And before I went into the ministry full time, I could pray for more than 20 hours a day."

If you want to last long in ministry, you must learn and practice long prayers. Don't wait for church activities to pray. Prayer is a personal deal with God. You might not have to pray as much as Jesus, but discipline yourself to pray while watching your increase (time spent in prayer).

Remember, you can pray anywhere, everywhere, and anytime.

I pray the Lord will transfer to you this special anointing for prayer and fasting. I pray the Lord will connect you with prayerful people.

Get up and start. Just take the first step, and the Holy Spirit will carry you, even if you have nothing to say or do not know what to say.

**Improve your service to God at church and daily.**

You are saved to serve God. When Moses went to speak to Pharaoh the very first time, he told him:

*So I say to you, let My son go that he may serve Me. But if you refuse to let him go, indeed I will kill your son, your firstborn.* — *Exodus 4:23*

Our original purpose on earth was to praise, worship, and serve God.

Serving God means to be available for Him. Whatever skill, gift, and talent you were born with, make them available to God for His glory and people.

Serving God is to serve people. Believe it or not, your servanthood is questionable if you do not minister to other people. God uses humans to bless humans, as well as using people to test people. That is his principle.

For his spiritual gift and ministry to be visible and mature, a new convert will have to serve in any department of his church. Yes, any department. As you serve, you grow, you learn, and the Lord can trust you with higher assignments and tasks. As you serve at your local church, you win trust. Remember, many are called, but few are chosen. God called many people for such work, but few will stick to the call. Few will serve God faithfully and honestly. Many will blow off the call for many reasons (pride, laziness, self-righteousness, etc.).

At every moment in the department of the church where you serve, be outstanding.

Before becoming the king of Israel, David served his father faithfully by defending his father's sheep against the lion and the bear.

Remember, the church is the place you come to serve and get served. Church is the place where you come to challenge and be challenged. There is nothing greater than to serve others. Our master Jesus, though he was a king, ministered on earth like a servant.

*But he who is greatest among you shall be your servant.* — *Matthew 23:11*

Service is the way to greatness. Service is the root of great leadership. Service is a way of blessing. It is a divine principle of the kingdom. Everyone making his first steps in the kingdom of heaven must have the ideology of service.

*~~~ Do the work of God faithfully and defend God's interest ~~~*

You cannot start serving God on the streets or at home. You will need to be at church. You must find a good Bible-based church that believes in holy doctrine such as water baptism, speaking in tongues, healing, and deliverance in Jesus' name. Once you find a good church by God's grace, do not leave. Stay and grow. From there, you will learn to serve your community and your nation.

*~~~ I pray the Lord sends you into a good*
*assembly for your spiritual growth ~~~*

Do not be a church-hopping Christian, changing your church every year. As much as you can, try to be a covenant member of a church. By experience, I have understood that we are mostly the reason we are not blessed. It is not because of the pastor, the church, or anybody else.

Once you begin to serve in your local church, improve yourself daily. No one can be perfect, but everyone can be excellent. Let everyone call you a good and faithful servant as it is written:

*Well done, good and faithful servant; you have been faithful over a few things...* — *Matthew 25:23*

Try your best to be at every church activity as much as your schedule allows. Try to be on time at church programs. Being on time shows your level of commitment, and it shows respect for yourself and toward others. People are not blind. They know and see whether you are improving. God made it that way.

On top of seeking improvement, you must serve God with joy. Do not be part of those who serve God muttering about God, the pastor, a member of the church, or the way the daily affairs of the church are run. When you mutter and grumble, you miss your blessing. Let the joy of God overflow. It will help you not to be discouraged when everything is not going well in your life. The joy through which you operate will contaminate your churchmates. This vibe always attracts people around you. Life is hard, but church should be fun, too. Servants of God should be envied by others called to serve God. When you make the service of God sound complicated and hard, it scares people away. All this is part of improving your service before God.

Your service before God includes your giving. Give with joy. Sow your seed into the church. Do not let your church lack anything. Participate financially in the economic foundation of the church. Pay your tithe. Pay the rent if possible.

The Bible says:

*And now my head shall be lifted up above my enemies all around me; Therefore, I will offer sacrifices of joy in His tabernacle; I will sing, yes, I will sing praises to the Lord. — Psalm 27:6*

The reward of serving God is huge. Your head shall be lifted above the enemies around you because you serve God. Then you shall offer sacrifices of joy in his tabernacle, meaning his house and temple. As you serve God, sing praise to the Lord even during tribulation.

At times, we are satisfied with what we have accomplished. If we get compliments from the pastor or the people, we tend to slack off. That should not be your case. The Bible teaches us to go from glory to glory. This must be applied to every aspect of our life. Serve God, I beseech you. Do not wait to hold the microphone like the pastor to serve God. If you do not know how to serve God or what to do, approach your pastor or an elder and ask. He will assign you to a task in the church.

*~~~Beloved, always fight against the storm and the devil, seek improvement in your service before God ~~~*

**Remove mediocrity and negligence from your habits.**

*Cursed is he who does the work of the Lord deceitfully, And cursed is he who keeps back his sword from blood. — Jeremiah 48:10 It is a fearful thing to fall into the hands of the living God. — Hebrew 10:31*

We are all creatures of habit. A slight positive or negative change in your habits can have a great positive or negative impact on your life. Your habits can become your character. Like they say: "We are what we repeatedly do." No one can live without a routine. If you make mediocrity, negligence, or even excuses your habit, you might not go too far in life with God.

I was taught by my spiritual father about negligence and mediocrity. These two adjectives are insults before God. He who wants to progress in life must remove them from his character. That must not define you.

*Mediocre* is defined as something of only moderate quality, not very good.

*Negligence* is defined as a failure to take proper care in doing something.

Would God be happy to see you not taking proper care of His properties? Do you think it will be suitable for God to offer Him something of poor quality? I do not think so.

God is holy, and everything that concerns Him must be so. A synonym of deceitful is negligence. The Bible teaches that it attracts a curse. When there is negligence in what you do, your life attracts a curse. You are removing any reason for God to bless you. It is not God cursing you; you are cursing your own life by your actions.

Beloved, let us work in a new dimension, at a new level. Meditate instead on the image of our master, Jesus Christ, with the help of the Holy Spirit, who knows the mind of God and gives strength to us in times of weakness. Let us build good habits of professionalism, seriousness, and total dedication. God help us.

Some mistakes are unpardonable, and mediocrity and negligence are the gateway to stupid mistakes. Critique your performance while not being too hard on yourself. Allow yourself to make mistakes, but do not make it a habit.

*~~~ In the name of Jesus, I come out against any power of negligence and mediocrity in your Christian life and destroy them by the power of the Holy Ghost. ~~~*

# CHAPTER 3

# HAVE A SPIRITUAL GAUGE

A gauge is important in mechanical devices like a car's gas tank, which lets the driver know the remaining gas volume. That is very important when deciding whether to add more gas.

Almost any energy device will need a power level indicator indicating whether you should refuel.

Our spiritual life works the same way. There are days you feel energized, and there are days you will feel low. There must be an internal invisible and spiritual gauge that indicates whether you are OK. The Holy Spirit offers that grace. The devil will always come after you at times of weakness, not strength.

**Define spiritual gauge.**

We can define "spiritual gauge" as the spiritual ability the Holy Ghost gives to every believer to warn them about the variations (the ups and downs) of their spiritual life. It is also a spiritual sensitivity one develops to indicate physical and spiritual stability and health. Through his communion with the Holy Spirit, a believer must know whether he is OK at any specific time. In the next section, we will discuss knowing that you are not doing great spiritually and getting back on track. Just because you are a citizen of the kingdom of heaven doesn't mean everything in your life will always be great.

## How do you know when you are at the lowest point of your spiritual life?

I grew up at church. I have been in the church all my life, and I became a pastor. I have seen it all. I have met all types of Christians. I have learned to read Christians when they are not well and do not want to open up to anyone. The signs are very visible. However, it is one thing for people to notice the issue and another for you to notice the change in yourself. At times, it can be not easy.

Here is a list of signs to pay attention to:

- Be careful when you are *physically tired and drained*. The Holy Spirit is powerful, but a tired body cannot function well under the anointing. It is important to rest. The Spirit is willing, but the body is weak, Jesus said.

*...the Spirit indeed is willing, but the flesh is weak. — Matthew 26:41*

- Be careful when you are *overwhelmed* or mentally tired. A tired mind cannot make the right decisions.

*The Spirit of a man will sustain him in sickness,*
*But who can bear a broken spirit? — Proverbs 18:14*

- Be careful when you lose *happiness*. Happiness is a fruit of the Spirit, a key ingredient for your health. Even worldly people do everything they can to stay happy. Be cautious when something is taking your happiness away when you are no longer happy. Serving the Lord unhappily results in God's anger.

*Serve the Lord with gladness; come before His presence with singing. — Psalms 100:2*

- The direct cause of the challenges above is *sadness*. Sadness is the seed of the devil. Do not let it dwell in you. That is why you want to be careful when you are sorrowful, especially when it is prolonged or continuously in a sad mood.

*Anxiety in the heart of man causes depression,*
*But a good word makes it glad.* — *Proverbs 12:25*

Sadness generates sorrow, and prolonged sorrow births anxiety, leading to depression.

- Be careful when you are too *distracted*. Distraction takes your focus away from the essential things of your spiritual life. Distraction could come in many forms. Distraction is a very slick spirit. You might not know you are distracted until the Holy Spirit reveals it. Distractions could be too many TV shows, too many games (of all types), too many friends and nonsense talk, excessive food, or too many useless jokes. It could be a relationship that profits nothing and takes more from you than it adds to your life. As soon as you see these signs, redirect yourself correctly.

- Be careful when you no longer want to deal with church stuff, such as prayer time, bible studies, conferences, seminars, etc. It could be that the church hurts you or something happened that killed your fire. This could be the cause of low spiritual strength. Sometimes, you do not want to serve God for an unknown reason. Some people stop going to church. This would not be a problem if they went to another church, but instead, they would stay home and follow the service online. When you feel negative about church and people at church, you should open up to your pastor or an elder and pray about it. The devil is trying to pull you out of the church to quench your fire. Satan will always do anything to pull you out of a zone of protection.

*Not forsaking the assembling of ourselves together, as is the manner of some, but exhorting one another, and so much the more as you see the day approaching.* — *Hebrews 10:25*

- Be careful when you are *excessively frustrated*. Frustration can cause anger, which can be the mother of great change. When it is directed to the wrong circumstance, then it can be damaging. It would help to watch out when you are frustrated at your life, situation, or somebody else's. Frustration can be good but bad as well. It depends on the state of your mind as you are facing it. Weak people tend to let frustration take over too easily. Every Christian must be able to turn their frustration into something good, learn, and grow from it. As the Bible says:

*...that the genuineness of your faith, being much more precious than gold that perishes, though it is tested by fire, may be found to praise, honor, and glory at the revelation of Jesus Christ. — 1 Peter 1:7*

- Be careful when you cannot pray and fast as you used to. The enemy's goal is for you to slumber or go into a deep spiritual coma so he can have a gap, a doorway to enter your life. He knows that if you pray, you are stronger. He knows that if you fast and pray, you are unshakable and can stand victoriously in any situation. God speaks and reveals himself to Christians when they pray. Fasting and prayer are Christians' powerful spiritual weapons (we shall address this more in another section).

*Pray without ceasing. — 1 Thessalonians 5:17*

- Be careful when you feel heavy, and laziness takes over you. Those are small things we neglect but could be costly. The Bible says:

*The sluggard does not plow after the autumn, so he begs during the harvest and has nothing. — Proverbs 20:4.*

Laziness makes you open your Bible and then fall asleep; laziness makes you slumber at church during preaching. Laziness makes you feel bored at church during a sermon. Laziness makes you run away from personal prayer time and procrastinate. It makes you postpone major events in your life. Laziness makes you give many excuses for what you were supposed to do but have not done. God never uses lazy people.

*~I pray the Holy Ghost revives your mortal body and gives you energy to accomplish your mission effectively. ~~~*

- Be careful when you have too many uncontrolled fleshly desires. I would call these temptations. The enemy will send temptations of all kinds. He will send temptations you used to deal with, temptations you used to fight. These he will bring back. For instance, if you used to be an alcoholic, the enemy would use that smell of alcohol to open the door and put you under his power again. You ought to know these key signs and set about praying. That demon that left will come back to see if the house is full of the Holy Ghost. He will call seven other stronger demons and possess the Christian again if not. Then his present condition will be worse than before. It is important as a Christian to know exactly when temptation is coming.

For example, when your sexual desire is high, especially for singles, and when the enemy bombards your mind with dirty images, images of fantasy, and filthy images, use a time of fasting to kill your flesh so your soul and Spirit take over. If you entertain those thoughts for too long, they will control your flesh and push you to act just as you think.

*But I say to you that whoever looks at a woman to lust for her has already committed adultery with her in his heart. — Matthew 5:28*

*Finally, brethren, whatever things are true, whatever things are noble, whatever things are just, whatever things are pure, whatever things are lovely, whatever things are of good report, if there is any virtue and if there is anything praiseworthy—meditate on these things.— Philippians 4:8*

**Know when you need to be alone with God.**

I have given some key warning signs to look out for. It will help your spiritual gauge, and failure in your new Christian journey will be avoided. In this next section, I will give you some interesting points addressing when to go in your closet and pray, seeking God's face.

Jesus said:

*"But you, when you pray, go into your room, and when you have shut your door, pray to your Father who is in the secret place; and your Father who sees in secret will reward you openly."* — *Matthew 6:6*

The Bible says, *"when you pray,"* not *"if you pray."* Prayer is not a matter of condition but of the period and time of prayer. The question we should ask is, *why* should we pray? And *how* do you know when we should spend alone time with the Lord in a closet? You can know by answering the questions below.

- Do you feel like you are stagnating and not growing in your spiritual life?
- Do you have a lot of questions and incomprehension about ministry?
- Do you have any questions about your personal life?
- Do you feel lost in life?
- Do you want a divine direction?
- Do you want a relationship (Father-son/ Father-daughter) between you and God?
- Do you want to know God deeply?
- Do you want to have an encounter with God?
- Are you seeking a divine miracle?
- Is there a problem that bothers you, and you cannot open up to anyone?
- Is there something bubbling inside of you pushing you to pray?
- Do you have a strong urge for revival?
- Do you have a strong urge for prayer?
- Do you want God to use you in another dimension?
- Are you a leader in the ministry?
- Do you have a calling?
- Do you want to know your calling?
- And so on...

The list of questions is endless. For THESE questions, go in your closet.

You may ask me, "Pastor Eric, how often should I spend time alone with God?"

My answer is pure and simple: Every day!

Build that habit and let it become your second nature. One could ask: How long should I stay in my closet? Again, my answer is pure and simple: until you receive a clear answer from the Lord. If you have not received an answer, you must stop the prayer and return later to continue, and please continue.

Amen.

**Know when the Spirit is leading you to take a time of fasting.**

**Some ways to know the Spirit is leading you to fast:**

- If you lose your appetite, I recently discovered that losing your appetite does not necessarily mean you are sick. It could be a sign that God is pushing you to cut your bodily food needs to make it easy to refrain from food.
- When you notice that walls block your progress in life, fasting is like dynamite that busts any resistance.
- When you find out that every Christian you know is taking some fasting time.
- When your pastor calls for a general fast in the church.
- Suppose you have a dream that God is telling you too fast. This is called revealed fasting. Your obedience is the key to tapping into the blessing. This fasting type is easier regardless of length because God provides the strength to carry the task.
- When you have a strong desire to fast, the Holy Spirit usually puts that desire into your heart. He compels you to do so. If you obey, you will see the result.

**Know when you should be with people and when to leave.**

Jesus was a man of the crowd. He would teach the people for hours and hours. He would go to the synagogue all day. He would minister by the seashore. But I noticed that Jesus knows exactly when to leave the crowd — even his disciples — and spend alone time in prayer. Jesus would send the crowd away. There is no problem being with people, but if you spend too much time in the crowd, interacting continuously, it could be hard to hear from God and recharge your spiritual battery. Remember, a tired mind cannot make the right decisions. You cannot build a good relationship with God without a stronger relationship with people.

*Now, those who had eaten were about five thousand men, besides women and children. Immediately, Jesus made His disciples get into the boat and go before Him to the other side while He sent the multitudes away. And when He had sent the multitudes away, He went up on the mountain by Himself to pray.* — *Matthew 14:21-23*

Jesus performed a mighty miracle. The people were blessed. However, Jesus realized that His job was over, and now it was time to move on to the next assignment. Jesus didn't waste a minute. He dismissed his disciples, and He dismissed the crowd.

**~~~ I believe if anyone wants to grow and remain rooted in their faith, he should have the wisdom to know what and when the next mission is ~~~**

We all have friends, and a lot of them. Whether you are a pastor of 50 or thousands, you must be in the midst of the crowd like Jesus. With the help of your "spiritual gauge," you must know exactly when to temporarily leave the crowds to pray and reconnect with God.

**You must know when you are doing a little too much of something.**

*Dishonest scales are an abomination to the Lord,*
*But a just weight is His delight.* — *Proverbs 11:1*
*Honest weights and scales are the Lord's; All the weights in the bag are His work.* — *Proverbs 16:11*

A scale is an instrument used to determine the approximate or exact weight of something. A weight is a piece of solid iron used to determine the weight of something else by putting them both on a scale. There are ways to trick and cheat a scale. This is why the Lord says, "Dishonest scales are an abomination." The Lord hates injustice. As I grow, I understand that injustice is not only when one is unfair in his ways and actions but everything that is not done with equity, equality, impartiality, and parity. The bottom line is that the Lord dislikes everything that is overdone, especially when it is not Spirit-led. A little too much of one thing could be harmful. This is a call for Christians. Too many Christians are victims of Satan because they do too much of what is not of God. Because of that, they suffer severe consequences. There is always a red line never to cross and a red zone not to go into. Since most Christians need to learn how to listen to the Holy Spirit, their spiritual gauge could be more functional. They never notice when they are overdoing something. You must know when you are joking too much, oversleeping, playing too much, overeating, sinning too much, or overreacting. Did you love someone else more than yourself and God?

Remember that God loves "honest weights and scales." Therefore, be careful. Do the right thing and put God first. It is important to notice that one can never pray too much but can only pray too little. Let the people say amen!

**Know when you love the blessing more than the one who blesses.**

We all love blessings. We all want to be blessed. More than 99% of Christians attend church because they want to be blessed. There is nothing bad about it.

There are 3,573 promised blessings in the Bible. There are blessings concerning life, career, finances, job, family, health, and future.

*Now it shall come to pass, if you diligently obey the voice of the Lord your God, to observe carefully all His commandments which I command you today, that the Lord your God will set you high above all nations of the earth.*

*And all these blessings shall come upon you and overtake you because you obey the voice of the Lord your God. — Deuteronomy 28:1-2*

Blessings are a direct consequence of obedience and total submission to the principles of God. When do we say that the Lord blesses someone?

**~~~One is called blessed by the Lord when he
obeys God and follows His conditions. ~~~**

Blessings are important to mark the difference between the work of darkness and God. Blessings are important for people to know that your God is alive and real. Blessings are important for you to never regret believing in Jesus. Blessings are the portion of humanity, especially for those who follow the laws of God.

The Lord says:

*The Lord will command the blessing on you in your storehouses and in all to which you set your hand, and He will bless you in the land which the Lord your God is giving you. — Deuteronomy 28:8*

This is the promise of the Lord.

As years pass, we notice that Christians increasingly fight for their blessings. They pray, fast, and sow seeds, all so they can collect blessings from the Lord. There is a race in the spiritual realm for blessing. This is good, but there is better. Do not worship the blessing but worship the one who blesses. Loving only the blessing can take you away from the kingdom of heaven. If all your attention is on getting blessings, you will forget why you are in the kingdom.

Blessings are good; I want to be blessed, and I desire you to be blessed. But there is a better desire. If you want to be an efficient growing Christian and last long in your walk with the Lord, you must pay more attention to the one who blesses (God) and not to the blessings. You must look for the one who gives the blessing, not the blessing itself. You will need to look for what is in the mind of the one who blesses rather than looking for what is in the hands of God.

~~~**Brothers and sisters, seek the one who
blesses, not the blessings.** ~~~

**Don't be a Christian who seeks blessings more than God.**

By looking actively for blessings, you are exposing yourself to temptation.
You are exposing your life to danger by looking for material and perishable
stuff. You can be led astray quickly. The devil knows your first motivation
is material — money, cars, houses, etc. He will control you if he sends them
to you, knowing that you do not have discernment. I have seen people
blessed and taken away from God. The blessings perverted them. The
blessings pulled out character traits that were hidden deep in their souls.
Many brothers and sisters backslid while racing for blessings. Their faith
was quenched. They were seduced and died. They followed the blessings
too much and forgot the owner of all things. That is a tragedy. Receive
and celebrate the blessings of God, but do not worship them. Worship
God alone.

The Bible says:

*He made known His ways to Moses and His acts to the children of Israel. —
Psalm 103:7*

God showed His ways to Moses. By that, the Bible means that God showed
His mind to Moses. God revealed everything in His mind to Moses. God
showed some hidden secrets and visions He would not show the public.
God would call Moses out of the cloud and explain everything about the
Tabernacle's construction. However, when it comes to the people, the
crowd, the others, and the public, God would show His acts, miracles,
blessings, and deeds. From this verse, we understand that there are two
groups of people.

- Those who want to know the mind of God, understand His ways, and
find out about His character

- And those who do not care about His mind do not want any revelation but want the blessing, the miracle, God's acts. They want to stay on the surface.

~~~ *My friend, please seek the mind of God.* ~~~

Jesus said: *"It is finished!"* He paid the price. Now, we all can access the holy of holies behind the veil.

*Beloved brothers and sisters in Christ, it is good to be blessed, but we should seek the one who blesses more than blessings. You must know when you are seeking the blessing too much. The devil will present you a copy of blessings God had already prepared for you in the heavens. Discern and ask God's opinion. This will help you in your spiritual growth.*

**Avoid idolatry.**

We just spoke about not loving the blessing more than the person of Jesus. From there, we can define idolatry as "extreme admiration, love, or reverence for something or someone." Anything you love more than God is idolatry. And it is an unpardonable sin. If the Lord blessed you with a car, a house, or a business, and you love it more than God, it is called idolatry. If the Lord blessed you with a husband, a wife, or a child, and you end up loving them more than God, it is idolatry. God should be your only source of joy. No one and nothing else should.

When the order of worship is messed up, we have a dilemma.

Idolatry is not only when you worship a wooden, stony, handmade god. It is when you place anything in your heart at the very place where God should be.

~~~ **God first** ~~~

*"You shall have no other gods before Me.*

*"You shall not make for yourself a carved image—any likeness of anything that is in heaven above, or that is in the earth beneath, or that is in the water under the earth; you shall not bow down to them nor serve them. For I, the Lord your God, am a jealous God, visiting the iniquity of the fathers upon the children to the third and fourth generations of those who hate Me, but showing mercy to thousands, to those who love Me and keep My commandments. — Exodus 20:3-6*

*And you shall love the Lord your God with all your heart, with all your soul, with all your mind, and with all your strength. This is the first commandment. — Mark 12:30*

Avoid the idea of loving anything other than God. God is a jealous god. He wants the first place, not the second. Abraham loved his son Isaac so much that God had to test him. Please do not push God to test you with the blessings he gave you by allowing them to take over your whole mind to the point that you push God aside.

The Bible teaches us to guard our hearts. Therefore, guard your heart from idolatry.

I pray the Lord gives you the strength and wisdom to do so. It is very easy to fall into idolatry. You can love your job more than God to the point that you miss Sunday services for work. Every day, check yourself and make sure nothing is taking God's place in your heart. In this way, you will securely guarantee success in your new Christian journey.

# CHAPTER 4

# VERY IMPORTANT INGREDIENTS TO NEVER PLAY WITH

Besides the topics previously discussed, I want to add some important key ingredients so that you, the reader of this book, can be fully equipped and ready to stand your ground firmly, challenging the enemy and winning battles one by one.

## A life of meditation

Meditation is to think deeply or focus one's mind for a period of time, in silence or with the aid of chanting, for religious or spiritual purposes, or as a relaxation method. To meditate is also to think deeply or carefully about something. In Christianity, meditation is to spend time in quiet and silence while thinking deeply about the Bible or a verse to understand its meaning. Meditation also means to premeditate, to imagine using your mind. It means to visualize or create a mental visual of something, devise, picture in your mind, contrive, ponder, put something into practice, think deeply, or focus on the word of God. Meditating is to contemplate, think about something, and weigh up.

During meditation, it is important to shut away every noise and negative voices from the outside while opening your spiritual ears to hear from the Holy Spirit. Close your physical senses and open your spiritual senses, meaning your spiritual eyes and ears. Meditation is a very powerful tool to hear from God. It is good to receive divine inspiration. God usually speaks in times of silence and meditation. There are plenty of examples in the Bible. Meditation is a way to calm the storms inside you, bringing your emotions and feelings to rest. Calm and rest kill stress, depression, and anxiety.

Some people meditate on their fears, mistakes, failures, getting sick, etc. That is why they have bad dreams. They sit all day and think of everything bad. They think about how people do not love them and how no one treats them as they should have. Some people meditate on how things will turn bad. At some point, we all meditated more on the bad than the good things.

*For thus says the Lord God, the Holy One of Israel: In returning and rest you shall be saved; In quietness and confidence shall be your strength. — Isaiah 30:15*

The Lord is saying to Israel — meaning you, the Christian — that your strength and power come or are awakened when you are quiet and confident. When you are not confident and quiet, you lose mental stability and your identity in Christ; you open a door for the devil to sneak into your life. Lack of confidence and quietness leads to a total loss of faith in Christ Jesus. And without faith, no one can please God.

*Then Jacob was left alone, and a Man wrestled with him until the breaking of day. — Genesis 32:24*

*And Isaac went out to meditate in the field in the evening, and he lifted his eyes and looked; there, the camels were coming. — Genesis 24:63*

When Jacob was left alone, the angel came and fought with him to release the blessing. Isaac met his future wife in the evening time of meditation.

*~~~My advice to every single man is to learn to meditate before entering into marriage~~~*

A newborn Christian should practice meditation. Remain quiet and silent while reading the Bible. It is amazing how, nowadays, Christians do not know the scripture. They cannot quote one single verse of the Bible with references. It is sad. The devil works best in the ignorance of Christians.

*~~My people perish because of lack of knowledge — Hosea 4:6 ~~*

You can only be and manifest what you know. And what you know from the Bible builds up your spiritual identity. The Bible says:

*Now, I say that the heir, as long as he is a child, does not differ from an enslaved person, though he is master of all. — Galatians 4:1*

You can be a child physically, but you can also be a child spiritually. That is even more disastrous.

If you are reading this portion of the book, please pause and ask yourself: How well do I know the Bible? What is my response to the devil using the Bible whenever he comes at me?

The Bible is everywhere nowadays, on smartphones, tablets, and computers. Most of the different versions are free. Christians must read and meditate on the Bible daily.

An empty stomach eats any given food. An empty Christian stomach will slowly eat any devilish doctrine out there. That is a fact.

*In the first year of his reign, I, Daniel, understood by the books the number of the years specified by the word of the Lord through Jeremiah the prophet, that He would accomplish seventy years in the desolations of Jerusalem. — Daniel 9:2*

When Daniel decided to read the book of the prophet Jeremiah (the Bible), he discovered the truth about the people of Israel and their liberation from captivity in Babylon. Can you imagine if Daniel hadn't read the book of Jeremiah? He wouldn't have discovered the promise of liberation or begun fasting and interceding, and the people of Israel could have been in captivity for more than 70 years.

### ～～～ Read and meditate on your Bible, and you will discover secrets about your future ～～～

As you read and meditate on the scripture, you acquire knowledge. The application of knowledge is called wisdom.

### ～～～The more you know, the wiser you become ～～～

That is why the Bible says:

*This Book of the Law shall not depart from your mouth, but you shall meditate in it day and night, that you may observe to do according to all that is written in it. For then you will make your way prosperous, and then you will have good success. — Joshua 1:8*

The Lord strongly advised Joshua that..

- The book of Law must not depart from his mouth
- He must meditate day and night (every day)
- And then obey everything that is written in it.

The consequences of these three key instructions offer three great heavenly blessings:

- A prosperous way
- Prosperity wherever he goes
- Success

As we continue reading the story of Joshua, we find out that he succeeded in all his battles (except one, the battle against Ai).

Beloved, it is undeniable that the Bible is the infallible word of God. It is powerful and necessary for the survival and daily growth of Christians.

Everything shall pass, but the word of God will never pass. In the beginning was the word, and everything was created by it…

Jesus won over the devil's temptations by using verses of the word of God He may have learned during his first 30 years. Three times He said, "It is written." (Luke 4:1-13)

*~~~What and where are your "it is written" ~~~*

Beloved brothers and sisters in Christ, read your Bible. It will sharpen your faith.

## Pray, Pray, and Pray

We will never say it enough in prayer. Prayer works. You cannot be an effective Christian without prayer. It is impossible.

The Bible says:

*Is anyone among you suffering? Let him pray. Is anyone cheerful? Let him sing psalms. Is anyone among you sick? Let him call for the elders of the church, and let them pray over him, anointing him with oil in the name of the Lord. And the prayer of faith will save the sick, and the Lord will raise him up. And if he has committed sins, he will be forgiven. Confess your trespasses to one another, and pray for one another, that you may be healed. The effective, fervent prayer of a righteous man avails much. Elijah was a man with a nature like ours, and he prayed earnestly that it would not rain, and it did not rain on the land for three years and six months. And he prayed again, and the heaven gave rain, and the earth produced its fruit. — James 5:13-18*

The Bible suggests that we should pray in any life situation, whether suffering, happiness, sickness, sin, or a brother in turmoil. Most people would complain and worry. Worries and complaints never solved problems. God knows exactly what we want, but he wants us to express it.

The principle of deities states that any given god is

-   to be prayed,
-   worshipped
-   served, studied
-   and sacrificed unto.

Therefore, you pray not because you want to ask God for many things, but you must pray because there is a God who can hear you.

Our God is the God of gods, so he must be prayed to daily. Prayer is important to talk to our God, Jehovah. God cannot do anything if you do not invite him. He does not violate our privacy. When it comes to the affairs of humans, God does not get involved unless he is invited.

As we defined before, prayer is the authorization humans give to God to intervene in their daily affairs. Yes, God needs your authorization before working on your behalf.

Beloved precious saints, the second pillar of the Islamic religion, states that every Islamic believer must pray five times a day. Hebrews pray three to four times a day. See how they respect and value to prayer. No wonder they are so blessed. They obey that principle systematically. Since praying is a principle, the consequences are positive if you respect it and negative if you do not.

You can pray anytime and anywhere during the day. You can talk to God, your father, in the name of Jesus Christ. You do not have to wait on the pastor.

You can pray to God lying on the bed, standing, kneeling on the floor, sitting on a chair, walking, running, or driving. God looks at your heart and faith, not how you dress. You can pray to God in any language you speak; God created all languages. You can tell God anything and everything that is in your heart without shyness. Tell Him everything. Let Him know how you feel and what you expect from him. Again, remember that He is our father. He is your father.

FIRST STEPS IN THE KINGDOM:

*Ask, and it will be given to you; seek, and you will find; knock, and it will be opened to you. — Matthew 7:7*

There are five types of prayer:

- Thanksgiving prayer: prayer to give thanks to the Lord
- Forgiveness prayer: Prayer to ask forgiveness of God for any sin committed willingly or unwillingly
- Intercessory prayer: Prayer to God on behalf of someone or a situation
- Prayer with a request: Prayer to ask anything you need of God (health, prosperity, breakthrough, etc.)
- Warfare prayer: Prayer where a believer is engaged in warfare against the devil and any wicked forces to cancel and destroy his plots and plans.

*For we do not wrestle against flesh and blood, but against principalities, against powers, against the rulers of the darkness of this age, against spiritual hosts of wickedness in the heavenly places. — Ephesians 6:13*

Beloved, prayer is the key. The more and longer you pray, the more information God downloads into your Spirit. The harder you pray; the more Satan is afraid of you. You can access mind-blowing miracles, which become easy for you.

*~~~ He who can talk to God can talk to anyone and in any situation~~~*

Prayer by faith moves mountains. Prayer destroys the works of Satan. Prayer gives peace to your soul. Prayer makes you prayerful. Prayer opens the windows of heaven.

A prayerless Christian is shameful for the body of Christ. You become cold and confused when you pray less. You lose even before spiritual battles begin. Prayer accelerates your blessings. Prayer makes you a friend of Jesus. Though God is God, God cannot move unless prayer is prayed. Practice prayer. Start even though you are heavy and do not know what to say.

## ~~~*Pray, my friends, pray* ~~~

*The fervent prayer of a righteous man avails much. — James 5:16*

*Watch and pray, lest you enter into temptation. The Spirit, indeed, is willing, but the flesh is weak. — Matthew 26:41*

Prayer helps you avoid temptation, enabling God's angels to guard you. Prayer fuels up angels and empowers them to carry on God's mission.

The more you pray, and God recognizes your voice, the more the spiritual realm knows you as a dangerous spiritual trader.

Never say, "I do not know what to say to God." Would you say the same thing when hanging out with your best friend? No. Therefore, do not say, "I have nothing to say to God." It is a statement of lazy people, an excuse not to pray.

If you find it too hard to pray, connect with a prayer partner or a friend who can pray so you can catch fire.

I have personally experienced the power of prayer on countless occasions. Today, I carry a life-changing testimony everywhere I go. To God be the glory. We are all, at some point, the product of prayer. Someone might have been praying for us even to be able to enter the kingdom of heaven. Who are you praying for?

Train yourself and build a habit of prayer. Start with 5 to 15 minutes a day, then increase. Keep it consistent and do that for 21 days straight. Next thing you know, you have built a good habit of prayer.

We could talk more about prayer in depth, but for you now, you need to understand that prayer is a must as you grow in Christ. Strengthen your relationship with the Lord in prayer.

**Fasting**

Fasting is to refrain from food for a certain period to devote time to prayer and spiritual activity. Fasting could be as short as one day. It could also be as long as 40 days. It is a lifetime business. Fasting removes any distraction and uncleanness and allows us to become holy to the Lord for some time. Most religions observe fasting and practice it. Many stories in the Bible show how lives and situations changed overnight because of the power of prayer.

If we want to become effective Christians, we must be able to fast. Sadly, most Christians I talk to these days ignore fasting, know little about fasting, or have never done it. No wonder the church, the body of Christ, is under Satan's heavy power. When we spend time eating, filling our stomachs with all types of junk food, we become less and less efficient in the spiritual realm. Remember, the more you eat, the weaker your fire will be.

On the other hand, the more you fast, the greater your fire. Fasting kills your flesh and elevates your Spirit. For when the flesh is too heavy, it is hard to perceive the voice of God. I am what I am today because I understood and practiced fasting since childhood. I have seen witches and wizards fasting to gain more power and control over their bodies and spirits. If those unbelievers fast gain power, how about you, precious saints?

Fasting is like an atomic bomb that causes damage in the camp of the enemy. It stops any war, just like during World War II.

Since fasting can be a complicated exercise, you can start by not eating any breakfast. After your body is used to it, push it to skip lunch until sundown. As you reduce your food appetite, you subconsciously increase your spiritual appetite. They are inversely proportional.

Here is a list of stories in the Bible about the power and effect of fasting:

1. **To prepare for ministry.** Jesus spent 40 days and nights in the wilderness fasting and praying before He began God's work. He

needed time alone to prepare for what His Father had called Him to do. During His fasting, I am supposing that he drank water. Water is not food because it does not contain any vitamins or protein. *(Matthew 4:1-17; Mark 1:12-13; Luke 4:1-14)*

*Then Jesus, being filled with the Holy Spirit, returned from the Jordan and was led by the Spirit into the wilderness. — Luke 4:1*

2. **To seek God's wisdom.** Paul and Barnabas prayed and fasted for the elders of the churches before committing them to the Lord for His service. They prayed probably that the Lord would guide them in the newly built church and that the Lord would give them wisdom to take care of His sheep. And that happened during fasting.

*So, when they had appointed elders in every church and prayed with fasting, they commended them to the Lord in whom they had believed. — Acts 14:23*

3. **To show grief.** Nehemiah mourned, fasted, and prayed when he learned Jerusalem's walls had been broken down, leaving the Israelites vulnerable and disgraced. Nehemiah was in pain. He lamented because the house of God was not in shape. It was broken down. Sometimes, I wonder how many people now would care about the house and the work of God so much that they would go into a time of fasting and prayer. The yoke, the burden, and the burning desire to do something about this situation were in his heart. However, he could not do anything before crying to the Lord in praying and fasting.

*So it was, when I heard these words, that I sat down and wept and mourned for many days; I was fasting and praying before the God of heaven. — Nehemiah 1:4*

4. **To seek deliverance or protection.** Ezra declared a corporate fast and prayed for a safe journey for the Israelites as they made the 900-mile trek to Jerusalem from Babylon. Do you know that a whole country can decree a fasting day for God to deliver and bless the country? I wish some president and political leaders would do so. Amen!

Nehemiah fasted with his people for protection during the journey, and God answered. Amen, amen, and amen!

*Then I proclaimed a fast there at the river of Ahava, that we might humble ourselves before our God, to seek from Him the right way for us and our little ones and all our possessions. For I was ashamed to request of the king an escort of soldiers and horsemen to help us against the enemy on the road because we had spoken to the king, saying, "The hand of our God is upon all those for good who seek Him, but His power and His wrath are against all those who forsake Him."*

*So, we fasted and entreated our God for this, and He answered our prayer.*
— *Ezra 8:21-23*

5.  **To repent.** After Jonah pronounced judgment against the city of Nineveh, the king covered himself with sackcloth and sat in the dust. He then ordered the people to fast and pray. Nineveh was a sinful city. They had to call a corporate fast to calm God's wrath, humble themselves, and repent. This worked because God showed mercy. As a Christian, if you have sinned, you can fast as an act of repentance, and He will forgive you.

*When God saw what they did and how they turned from their evil ways, He relented and did not bring on them the destruction He had threatened. — Jonah 3:10*

6.  **To gain victory.** After losing 40,000 men in battle in two days, the Israelites asked God for help. They also "fasted that day until evening." The next day, the Lord gave them victory over the Benjaminites. The Lord can give you victory over the demons, witches, and wizards when you fast and fight them. We have experienced it many times. Some deliverances only happen when Christians fast. Jesus said, "*This type of demon comes out only by fasting.*"

*Then all the children of Israel, that is, all the people, went up and came to the house of God and wept. They sat there before the Lord and fasted that day until evening, and they offered burnt offerings and peace offerings before the Lord.*

*So, the children of Israel inquired of the Lord (the ark of the covenant of God was there in those days, and Phinehas the son of Eleazar, the son of Aaron, stood before it in those day, saying, "Shall I yet again go out to battle against the children of my brother Benjamin, or shall I cease?"*

*And the Lord said, "Go up, for tomorrow I will deliver them into your hand.*
*— Judges 20:26-28*

7. **To worship God.** Luke 2 tells the story of an 84-year-old prophetess named Anna. Verse 37 says, "She never left the temple but worshiped night and day, fasting and praying." Anna was devoted to God, and fasting expressed her love for Him. I am calling every worshipper and gospel singer to practice fasting. Fast until God pours His anointing on you to worship Him like the 24 elders. We have turned our face to skills and talent, and we neglect that seeking God's face is the secret of a long-standing and sharp anointing.

*… and this woman was a widow of about 84 years, who did not depart from the temple but served God with fasting and prayers night and day. — Luke 2:37*

Dr. Bill Bright, founder of Campus Crusade for Christ, firmly believed in the power of prayer and fasting. In his guide, *Why You Should Fast*, he listed the reasons for seeking God through self-denial.

- Fasting was an expected discipline in both the Old and New Testament eras.
- Fasting and prayer can restore the loss of the "first love" for your Lord and result in a more intimate relationship with Christ.
- Fasting is a biblical way to humble yourself in the sight of God.
- Fasting enables the Holy Spirit to reveal your spiritual condition, resulting in brokenness, repentance, and a transformed life.
- Fasting will encourage the Holy Spirit to quicken the Word of God in your heart, and His truth will become more meaningful to you.
- Fasting can transform your prayer life into a richer and more personal experience.

- Fasting can result in a dynamic personal revival in your life and make you a channel of revival to others.

We often don't fast because we've lost our spiritual appetite. John Piper says, "The absence of fasting is the measure of our contentment with the absence of Christ."

Piper adds, "If we don't feel strong desires for the manifestation of the glory of God, it is not because we have drunk deeply and are satisfied. It is because we have nibbled so long at the table of the world. Our soul is stuffed with small things, and there is no room for the great."

*~~ fasting is a much-needed discipline in the life of a believer~~*

## Participation in the growth of your local church

As we spoke briefly in the previous sections, a new Christian should be serving God. You are saved to serve God, first in your local church, then everywhere you go. A new Christian must have a burning fire and desire to see their church growing in all aspects. You must put your soul into the development of your church. You must embrace the vision of the leader. It would help if you worked side by side with him. Beloved, there should be a burning desire to see your loved church growing and in the future. It is an unexplainable feeling.

Here is a set of questions I ask of newborn Christians:

- How badly do you love your church?
- How well do you know the vision and the mission of the church?
- How well do you know your church's culture?
- How much are you in agreement with your spiritual leader and his vision?
- How much do you want to see your church blessed?
- How much do you want your church to grow numerically?
- How much are you ready to put into every event of your church?

- Does your church come after your relationship with God and your family?

(In some cases)

These are just a few questions you should ask yourself. All the answers should be positive.

I, Pastor Eric, refuse the shutting down of a church. Members can leave the church; we have seen it throughout its story. However, a church of God, the house of God, closing? That is an insult to God, a tragedy. It is a no. It must not happen. If two people in the building pray and fast, the church should not close. The church could relocate to a smaller or bigger facility depending on the vision and their needs but not close.

Do you know that Satan rejoices and has a feast when a new Christian backslides?

Do you know that at least ten clubs and bars open when a church closes?

*~~~I am encouraging every Christian member of any given church, old or new Christians, to please support their church wisely, financially, spiritually, and physically so it will continue to fulfill its kingdom mandate~~~*

Anywhere the Holy Spirit is, there must be growth and unity. God will add to that which is already running. Let's have that in our minds and be serious about the church of God.

*…praising God and having favor with all the people. And the Lord added to the church daily those who were being saved. — Acts 2:47*

As a new citizen of the kingdom of heaven, find a local church and serve there.

*~~~ If you are not serving God, you will serve the devil~~*

Participate in the growth of your local church by doing these:

- **Always speak well about your church.** Remember that if you live on Earth, you will never find a perfect church because no one is perfect. I usually say that church is a gathering of sick people seeking grace and mercy.
- **Speak well about your pastor.** Learn to cover his flaws even when everybody speaks badly about him. At the end of the day, people come to church and stay not because of the building but because of the anointing on the head. If a bad reputation and gossip kill the head, the sheep (weak in soul) will scatter.
- **Advertise your church.** How can you fellowship in a church and then turn around and disgrace this church by discouraging people from coming? Why are you still coming to the church then? Do not speak badly about your church, especially to the unbelievers. In this age of social media, everyone posts whatever they think. Do not post negative statements about your church.
- **Invite people all the time at your church for Sunday and weekly service. Spread information about any revival going on in the church.** I have heard some people saying stuff that broke my heart. They say, "I do want to invite people to my church because I don't like the way things are run." If you are frustrated about how things are being run in your congregation, pray about it or address it with your leader. Don't begin a negative campaign, or you might become a destructive agent Satan uses against the church.
- **Call and check on the people you do not see at church for a while.** Nowadays, Christians are extremely selfish. They mostly care about their blessings and well-being. When it comes to their neighbors, they do not care. If you want to see your church growing, visit and call a brother or sister you haven't seen for quite a while. Please do not do so only for those you like, but for everyone as soon as you notice they have been missing. It is unpleasant for a pastor to see that this task is left to him and his wife.
- **Pray and fast regularly for your church and its leaders:** In his writing, the apostle Paul requested prayer from saints.

*...and pray also for me, that utterance may be given to me, that I may open my mouth boldly to make known the mystery of the gospel. — Ephesians 6:19"*

Fast and pray to lead the battle against any destructive agents of your church. Do not follow the crowd of gossipers, but be the one who carries the burden for development in the church. Be zealous, interceding for your pastor so that his anointing may remain fresh and intact. Pray also for his growth, for as he grows, the church likely will grow.

## Service at church and your spiritual parents

We spoke about this in the previous section, but I will try to be more explanatory in this special section.

There is a secret in serving God that I discovered over the years. Anyone, even animals assigned a mission for the Lord, is automatically covered, protected, and guarded by God. As long as he remains obedient to God, God will always be there for him. We are in trouble only because we are always rebellious. We do not want to do His work. Do the work of God, and blessings will follow you. As the Bible says:

*Blessed are those servants whom the master, when he comes, will find watching. Assuredly, I say to you that he will gird himself and have them sit down to eat, and will come and serve them. — Luke 12:37*

*The Lord redeems the souls of His servants, and none of those who trust in Him shall be condemned. — Psalm 34:22*

*Mark the blameless man and observe the upright;*
*For the future of that man is peace.*
*But the transgressors shall be destroyed together;*
*The future of the wicked shall be cut off.*
*But the salvation of the righteous is from the Lord;*
*He is their strength in times of trouble.*
*And the Lord shall help them and deliver them;*
*He shall deliver them from the wicked,*

*And save them,*
*Because they trust in Him. — Psalm 37:37-40*

**~~Beloved, if you serve God with fear, He will always defend you from evil. Always! ~~~**

King David was a servant of God according to God's heart. King Saul sought for him to die, but the Lord never delivered him into the hands of Saul.

**~~~There is divine protection as you serve Jehovah Jireh ~~~**

God fights for his servants and does not let anyone harm them. As it is written:

*Do not touch My anointed ones, and do My prophets no harm. — 1 Chronicles 16:22*

Problems may come, sickness may come, Satan may attack, but God will lift you above the troubles. There are thousands of promises in the Bible concerning the servants of God. Many stories in the Bible of people, kings, and countries that served God and were saved when the enemy encompassed them.

There is also one thing that I would like to correct. Many saints think that God must bless them first, and then they will fully give themselves to serving God. Once everything is OK and full of money, goods, and blessings, they will serve God. It is a lie. It is impossible. It used to be my way of thinking. God does not work that way. God has principles, and he is the greatest businessman of all time. He will increase your blessings as you walk with him. He will open doors of blessing and opportunities as you serve him.

God called Abraham and said:

*Now the Lord had said to Abram:*
*"Get out of your country,*

*From your family*
*And from your father's house,*
*To a land that I will show you.*
*I will make you a great nation;*
*I will bless you*
*And make your name great;*
*And you shall be a blessing.*
*I will bless those who bless you,*
*And I will curse him who curses you;*
*And in you, all the families of the earth shall be blessed.* — *Genesis 12:1-3*

God told Abraham, "Leave your country and your family. Do my work first, and then I will bless you with such and such blessing." That is how God worked. There is no debate about it, no negotiation.

~~~ **Serve God, and he will serve you. Do his work, and then he will bless you, not the other way around** ~~~

To all my people making their first steps in the kingdom, find something to do at your local church. Serve in any department, getting busy for God in the name of the Lord. As you do so, little by little, every ancient gate in your life that remained closed will be opened. You are writing your story in the Book of Life as you serve Him. You are building an altar that will speak on your behalf when tough times come, nourished by your constant sacrifices in the house of God. God is my witness, and I am not lying. I live what I preach. I am writing based on my own experience. God blessed me because I understood at a very early age that principle.

Again, serve God. Find something to do at church. Whether big or small, do something. Join a department and be a covenant partner of your local church.

God will use people to bless you, especially your spiritual father and leader. If you want God to promote you, you must serve under somebody. It is the same rule as if you were working at a company. Serving God begins with serving people, and the first person to serve is your pastor, your spiritual father, or your spiritual leader. You cannot grow on your own. God will watch how you treat and serve under your leader. God will watch how humble, obedient, respectful, and available you are toward your spiritual father. We will discuss the spiritual father in the next sections.

*~~~ The anointing you honor will honor you. The anointing*
*you fight will combat you sooner or later ~~~*

**Participate in weekly church programs and special programs.**

Weekly programs are very important. Most Christians would just come on Sunday service (10 a.m.-noon). Guess what? It is not enough. Sunday service is just two hours, with a 45-minute sermon that is usually rushed because people must go home and rest to return to their busy lives in the coming week. You listen to the sermon during Sunday service and cannot ask questions. It is not enough at all for a newborn Christian to grow. You must attend bible studies as much as your schedule allows you. It is a time when you can ask questions. You need to remember:

**~~~ time spent in the house of God is never wasted~~~**

Therefore, spend much of your time at church. It is protection, a place where you stay out of trouble. That is why David says:

*One thing I have desired of the Lord,*
*That will I seek:*
*That I may dwell in the house of the Lord*
*All the days of my life,*
*To behold the beauty of the Lord,*
*And to inquire in His temple. — Psalm 27:4*

David desires to spend his whole life in the Lord's house to contemplate the Lord's beauty and wonderfulness. He knows that when away from the house of God, he runs straight into the enemy's hands. The house of the Lord is a hiding place. So, do not listen to people who argue that churches are places of drama. If you interact with people, there will be human reactions. Disregard the drama and focus on God and your growth. You must know why you are going to church. Like I always say, if you do not know why you are attending church, you might as well not go. Know where you go to church. Know what you are looking for. The answer to these two questions will keep you focused on your spiritual path.

*For a day in Your courts is better than a thousand.*
*I would rather be a doorkeeper in the house of my God*
*Then dwell in the tents of wickedness. — Psalm 84:10*

David is saying he wants to stand at the door of the house of God. To be an usher or a security guard in the house of the Lord will be more than enough for him. What a level of humility. No wonder he was a man according to God's heart.

*~~~ It is better to sweep the floor of the church than*
*to sweep the floor of the president's house~~~*

People have no idea of the blessings you get in return when you take care of the church or participate in the day-to-day activities of the house of God.

Stand up and participate whenever there is a revival, concert, fundraising, Christmas, or Easter program. You are making yourself be noticed by God, his angels, and even people. People of God, please know how to attract favor before God and people's eyes.

**Pay your tithe and offering.**

How can you be converted, but your wallet is not? How can you be Christian, but your purse is not? How can you be a kingdom citizen when your pocket is not?

A good convert in the kingdom of God should not be forced to pay tithe and give an offering. It should be printed on your DNA. You must know that you must pay your tithe. There is no discussion about it.

Christians usually forget to ask themselves these questions:

- How is the rent or mortgage of the church paid?

- How does the pastor pay the rent of the church?
- How much is the monthly utility bill?
- How do we pay for the church instruments and materials?
- Where do we get the funds to organize events in the church?
- How do the pastor and his family live?

Do not assume that someone else is going to bless the church. I have seen people think the church is financially stable because the church is big and has a couple of rich families. No, it is wrong to think like that. I am a pastor, and I know the cost of maintenance of a church. I know how expensive it is to keep a church running. It is one of the biggest headaches a pastor must go through. It might not be noticeable, but the struggle is real.

Nowadays, if a pastor teaches and exhorts people to pay their tithe, he is judged and called a greedy pastor. He is, therefore, obligated to shut his mouth and look at God until He pushes someone to take care of the expenses of the church. Indeed, God will always provide for the vision. But for your own sake, you must be a giver and a sower.

Though some pastors teach about tithes and offerings to get rich and live in luxury, it doesn't mean the doctrine of tithes and offerings is erroneous and that all pastors are the same.

To help everyone reading this book and any new convert holding it in their hands, let us go ahead and answer some questions to enlighten our spirits on tithes and offerings. However, we might only cover some biblical and spiritual explanations.

**1- What is tithe? What is offering?**

The Hebrew word for tithe is Mahasayr or Mahasraw. It is one-tenth of annual produce or earnings, formerly taken as a tax for the support of the church and clergy. A 10th of the produce of the Earth was consecrated and set apart for special purposes. The dedication of a 10th to God was recognized as a duty before the time of Moses. Abraham paid tithes to Melchizedek *(Genesis 14:20; Hebrews 7:6). Jacob* vowed unto the Lord and said, *"Of all that thou shalt give me, I will surely give the tenth unto thee."* Your tithe is the consecrated (set apart) portion of God in your income.

Every kingdom has a tax system. Every country has a tax system. Violation of the tax code can result in severe consequences. Our kingdom's tax system is only 10% of your income.

An offering is a thing offered, especially as a gift or contribution to God. There are five types of offerings in the Bible: guilt offering, burnt offering, sin offering, peace offering, and grain offering.

**2- What are my tithe and my offering for?**

You must pay your tithe and give your offerings for the biblical reasons listed below:

- To support the Levites and the priest caring for the house of God. Who are the Levites and the priests? They are the ministers, pastors, evangelists, apostles, and doctors working full-time day and night to care for the sheep and the house of God. They are the ones whom God uses to save souls and stand in the gap for the ongoing work of God.
- To take care of the house of God. I cannot admit personally that a church closes because the pastor cannot pay the rent and bills.
- Tithes and offerings are also for the maintenance of the church, sound system, air conditioner, plumbing, and electricity...
- To care for widows, widowers, orphans, and people experiencing poverty. Some people, now and then, face challenges where they need financial support. The church must be able to meet their needs and give them the minimum to sustain themselves.
- To organize conferences, seminaries, and any Christian gatherings like concerts and praise and worship nights.
- To support the different sub-ministries of the church: women's ministry, men's ministry, children's program...

**3- Where and when should I pay my tithe?**

The Bible says, "Bring your tithe into the storehouse," the storehouse is nothing but the house of God, where the church puts its food supplies. Since tithes are usually monetary, the storehouse refers to the savings account. It is the money the church sets aside to take care of the daily needs of the house of God. The Bible says, "So there will be food in the house of the Lord." Your tithe helps greatly in maintaining and supplying the house of God. Therefore, you give your tithes at the church, in the church's basket. You should bring your tithe every time you have an income during Sunday services and weekly programs.

*8 "Will a man rob God?*
*Yet you have robbed Me!*
*But you say,*
*'In what way have we robbed You?'*
*In tithes and offerings.*
*9 You are cursed with a curse,*
*For you have robbed Me,*
*Even this whole nation.*
*10 Bring all the tithes into the storehouse,*
*That there may be food in My house,*
*And try Me now in this,"*
*Says the Lord of hosts,*
*"If I will not open for you the windows of heaven*
*And pour out for you such blessing*
*That there will not be room enough to receive it." — Malachi 3:8-10*

**4- What blessing will I get when I pay my tithe?**

When you pay your tithe, God promises numerous blessings:

- God will open the floodgates of heaven and pour out so much blessing that there will not be room enough to store it.
- The Lord will prevent pests from devouring your crops, income, and any source of income.

- God will spare you from unnecessary, unplanned expenses sent by the devil to make you waste money.
- Any satanic money-wasting agent will be kept away from your house.
- The vines in your fields will only drop their fruit after it is ripe.
- All the nations will call you blessed.
- The Lord will prepare a delightful land for you.
- The Lord will prepare a secure future for your offspring.
- The Lord will give you grace to increase, multiply, and be fruitful in the land.
- Financial difficulties may come, but the Lord will take you through without harm.

*...and they shall not appear before the Lord empty-handed. — Deuteronomy 16:16*

Every Christian should understand that just because salvation is free doesn't mean that taking care of the house of God is free.

Remember what Apostle Paul said:

*So, let each one give as he purposes in his heart, not grudgingly or of necessity; for God loves a cheerful giver. — 2 Corinthians 9:7*

Do not listen to people who urge Christians not to give at the church. They sometimes say that you are giving to the pastor so he can be richer, and you become poorer. Those are demonic statements that prevent church growth, slow the gospel, and prevent the saints from being blessed. The work of God costs money.

Be a giver, be a tither.

Think about it. How much richer did you get if you didn't pay your tithe? How many houses did you build or buy? Paying your tithe and giving offerings is not to bribe God. They do not make God any richer. Gold, money, and silver belong to him. You give for yourself.

**Take discipleship and foundation classes.**

Discipleship classes are lessons from the senior pastor or an elder in the church. They come in many modules. They help to establish strong Christian foundations and build unshakeable, incorruptible Christians. Jesus spent three and a half years with his disciples, teaching them many holy doctrines and instructing them to make disciples all over the nations.

I strongly believe that no one can change anybody. However, a well-taught Christian causes less trouble to the kingdom of heaven than a Sunday Christian who has no foundation whatsoever.

*A disciple is not above his teacher, but everyone who is perfectly trained will be like his teacher. — Luke 6:40*

I noticed in the Bible that Jesus would speak in parables to the crowd, the Pharisees, the high priests, and the Sadducees. But when it comes to his disciples, He would not talk to them in parables but clearly. Jesus taught his disciples how to pray, cast out demons, and even baptize. Discipleship classes are extremely important for a new Christian to know and master holy doctrines such as healing and deliverance, baptism in water, the Holy Ghost, and fire. I would strongly suggest disciple courses in every church. Brother and sister, let us be teachable and trainable. Let us sit down and learn. We must suck in every good teaching coming out of our spiritual leader.

The goal of foundation courses is to make one strong, stable, and to reinforce the believer's knowledge of the doctrine of Christianity. Like a tree rooted deep into the ground, making it hard to be uprooted by any storm, so must the strengthening be for you. The main purpose of foundation courses is to form good Christians who will be strengthened by the knowledge of sound doctrine and reach maturity.

Discipleship and the foundational course have many benefits (I covered them in the book New Convert's Foundational Courses).

**Be loyal, not only faithful.**

In this last time, we live, we have seen all types of Christians. Some are visitors. Others are members who do not want to help in any way but are experts in criticism. They criticize the pastor, the church, the choir, the ushers, the protocol — everything their eyes fall on. They are extremely disloyal to the pastor and the church. I advise any born-again Christian to be loyal to the church you attend. That way, you will experience the full blessing of the Lord. Your reward will be countless, and you will attract favor before men and God. Loyalty is needed much more in hard times than in good times. When everything is good, everybody seems to be loyal. But wait to see what happens when bad times come. I appreciate everyone who stayed with me during trouble, even those who supported me when I made mistakes. I was loyal to my church and my pastor in Africa until I came to the United States of America.

**What is loyalty?**

"Loyal" means to give or show firm and constant support or allegiance to a person or institution. The opposite of loyalty is disloyalty. You must be loyal to your church and pastor.

How can you be loyal, and how can you avoid disloyalty?

- Do not isolate yourself too much from the brothers and sisters.
- Do not have too much of an independent spirit.
- Don't be too passive when offended by one thing or someone. Respond to offenses wisely and politely, if you do not stay too indifferent.
- Always be happy around your leader, elder, or pastor.
- Do not be too critical of the occurrences in the church.
- Do not be involved with people against the church system or your pastor.
- Do not be the go-to person for church hurts, complainers, and gossipers.
- Do not despise your teacher, pastor, or church.
- Do not be rebellious.

- Be fully convinced in your heart about anything you are involved in.
- Be open to your pastor and let him know what is happening in your life.

In this chapter, I explained some key ingredients for growing strong, like a Chinese bamboo tree.

In the next chapter, we will address what we all do not like: pain, suffering, and other tests. Of course, we will explain what attitude to adopt while going through them. Loyalty is tested. If the person you are submitted to doesn't show signs of loyalty, your loyalty can be challenged. If loyalty is the culture of a church, this church will sustain many storms without suffering harm.

# CHAPTER 5

# READY TO FACE TESTS

Life is challenging. No one is exempt from trials. When the sun rises, it shines everywhere. No one can tell the sun, "Do not shine on me; I want to remain in darkness." When it rains, no one tells the rain, "Do not fall on me." The rain falls whether you are happy or not, whether you like it or not. Pain is pain. Pain does not care about your age or your religious beliefs. It attacks everyone. Everything on Earth is subject to tests. When a manufacturing company makes a product, it goes through a series of tests called quality tests or quality checks to ensure it meets all requirements to satisfy customers. Again, life takes work. Everybody goes through tough times. Just because you become a Christian does not mean your life will become easier. You may not like what I said, but God is a tester as much as He is a God that blesses and changes lives. Remember, the main purposes of God letting you go through life trials are:

- To create and grow faith in you.
- To sanctify and test your heart to follow God's laws.
- To push you to always count on him alone.
- To mature spiritually and mentally.
- To push you to know him better.
- To conform you to the image of Jesus Christ.

One thing is sure: God will always ensure that you come out of the test victorious because He is there with you.

*When you pass through the waters, I will be with you;*

*And through the rivers, they shall not overflow you. When you walk through the fire, you shall not be burned, Nor shall the flame scorch you. — Isaiah 43:2*

As a Christian, God looks at your heart and your life. He knows what can stand in the way of your blessings. He knows what can prevent you from entering heaven. He knows the spot of darkness in your life. Based on all these facts, He knows how and what to do to bring you closer to Him so that you can be a nice copy of the image of Jesus. You may face the test of humility or the pride test. Sometimes, people ask me, "Pastor, if God knows all things, why would He test me to make sure I love him?" The answer is simple: you are not tested for God. The tests you go through do not change or affect God. They affect you. The goal is to purify and refine your like pure gold. The goal is to prepare you for blessings.

## Humility/Pride test

God resists the proud but gives grace to the humble.

The Bible says:

*Likewise, you, younger people, submit yourselves to your elders. Yes, all of you be submissive to one another and be clothed with humility, for*
*God resists the proud,*
*But gives grace to the humble. — 1 Peter 5:5*

*Surely, He scorns the scornful,*
*But gives grace to the humble. — Proverbs 3:34*

He who is proud does not accept criticism and rebukes. He cannot submit to spiritual authorities. He cannot accept change. Proud people ultimately have a problem with humility. God gives grace to the humble and resists the proud. For God to change you, He will have to test you to cause you to be less proud and more humble. He will cause some situations that might require you to apologize even though you are right, to remain silent even though you can defend yourself, to see others as above you regardless of who you are in society and life, to respect the younger and the smallest and set them above you, to see yourself as lower and below everyone else.

As a new Christian, you should be aware that you must be humble as Christ Jesus our Lord is. Pride is a very villainous thing that sits in the flesh of every single one of us. It is the one demon that resists God and his power. God cannot bless anyone unless they humble themselves.

As you make your first steps in the kingdom, you will go through many situations in life that will humble you. Learn not to complain and turn to God. Tell yourself: "God, I thank you, for you have allowed this situation to humble me. Glory be to your name, Amen."

**Patience test**

In every church, Christians are in a sort of blessing race. All their prayer is for God to bless them, not in due time but quickly. Patience is a hard thing when you are aging. Patience is hard when everyone seems to be doing great but not you. Patience is a virtue of the Holy Spirit. It is the art of waiting on God. It means moving when God moves. It is to flow at the speed of God, depending on his agenda for your life. To be patient is to believe and live by God's timing.

The trap is to believe that just because a sister was married last week, every single sister should get married as fast as possible. We see a new generation of Christians that wants everything right now. They are not patient at all. They forget that God works in His time, and no one can press God. Brothers and sisters, be patient. God never forgets anyone. By not being patient and waiting on God, many saints fall into temptation from the devil. Wait for your turn. It takes patience for God to prepare your blessing. It takes patience even to enter the presence of God and receive an answer from God. As someone told me a while ago, God is slow and takes his time; you must be patient to bear his pace. Because of the inability of most Christians to wait on God, the Lord must prepare tests, so they will have to wait until they are ready to be blessed.

Yes, everybody will experience the waiting place of God, where you learn to wait. It is a place where God prepares you to reach your next level. Abraham had to wait 25 years to see the fulfillment of his promise, and Sarah waited alongside her husband to see the birth of Isaac. Jacob waited 20 years at his uncle's house to get his blessings. Joseph had to wait more than two years in jail before being the prime minister of Egypt and 12 years before what he saw in his dream was manifested.

You will surely crash your life if you cannot wait on God.

*~~ Time is another name of God, and patience is his virtue. ~~*

I pray in the name of Jesus Christ that the Lord allows you to wait on Him. I pray that the Holy Spirit gives you the ability to be patient.

*...knowing that the testing of your faith produces patience. — James 1:3*

*But those who wait on the Lord*
*Shall renew their strength;*
*They shall mount up with wings like eagles,*
*They shall run and not be weary,*
*They shall walk and not faint. — Isaiah 40:31*

**Money test**

I call this section the money test because I have seen that it is one of the most dangerous reasons why many Christians lose their faith, church, and calling. When the devil sees that a new Christian is zealous, very engaged at church, and committed to his spiritual life, he may face money issues that will make him get a second job, work overtime, and work on Sundays. There is nothing wrong with having a job, but there is a problem when money becomes your main goal. When you find yourself in that position, you are pulled away from the church and the gathering of other Christians. The consequences are dangerous.

The purpose of that test is to quench the new believer's fire by isolating him. The more you miss church activities, the more your zeal and fire fade, and the easier target you become for the devil. I always tell Christians: Regardless of your problem, do not leave the church except for prayer and fasting. The money test is so hard that sometimes you lack a penny to give as an offering. You may need to put your rent together. You could need to catch up in paying your bills. It could be hard to get gas or the bus. It could be hard for you to buy yourself food. When all this happens, do not worry. God is faithful, and it is just a test. God is teaching you how to manage your finances. Just watch how much he can provide for you. Always count on God in these situations. Something very important to not forget:

*~~~When God blesses you financially and your situation changes, do not run from the church; do not let the blessing take you away. Always remain faithful in lack or abundance. ~~~*

*He who is faithful in what is least is faithful also in much, and he who is unjust in what is least is unjust also in much. — Luke 16:10*

During a time of lack, God can inspire an idea or vision you will implement. It may be an idea that can change the world and your life.

As you go through this test, do not be seduced by other people's success. Do not take a shortcut. Do not sign a contract with the devil. Wait your turn patiently. God will open a door for you.

**Love and hate test.**

I call this section the love and hate test because as you attend your local church, grow up in Christ, and serve the Lord, one thing that will make you an outstanding Christian is what you carry in your heart: Love. During your relationship with the Lord, you will meet all kinds of people: some fake friends, some gossiping Christians, some backstabbers, and some mean and evil talkers. Remember, the church is a place for all sick people seeking healing. Among these people, you must shine, showing love and making a difference.

*A new commandment I give to you, that you love one another; as I have loved you, that you also love one another.*
*By this, all will know that you are My disciples if you have a love for one another. — John 13:34-35*

Jesus commanded his disciples to love one another just as he loved us. If you want to grow to become a perfectly trained disciple, you must learn to love. Love is the network connection system of the kingdom of God. It might not be easy to love the person you call sister or brother in Christ who hurts you constantly. However, it is a command to love. By showing love, you make them understand that you are a good example, copying exactly your master Jesus. It is amazing how the body of Christ and the church has become unsafe and dangerous because of some people's actions and judgmental attitudes.

A sister, one day told me, "Pastor, I am not coming to church anymore." I asked her why, and she replied: "I overheard someone at church talking bad about you, including the people from the church. That turned me off." She continued, "How can you publicly praise your pastor then speak evil about him in private? That is being fake." Well, for this victimized Christian, I could only heal the damage by encouraging her, not justifying the wrong action. I begged her not to leave the church, but the damage was already done.

That is exactly why I am writing this book: to prevent Christians from falling into the enemy's trap and prepare a safe environment for their spiritual growth.

*For God so loved the world that He gave His only begotten Son, that whoever believes in Him should not perish but have everlasting life. — John 3:16*

***~~~If you want to be a good servant of God and see your anointing growing every day, show love to everyone~~~***

## Holiness

As we go in this section, we mean by holiness every characteristic of the holiness of God in you. God wants us to be holy, meaning to avoid all types of sin.

*...because it is written, "Be holy, for I am holy."— 1 Peter 1:16*

Some sisters did so well at the beginning of the conversion. They were on fire, doing everything in the church. Their zeal was so glorious. They were examples in the church. Sadly, because of their strong desire to get married and their inability to control their flesh and sexual drive, they fell into the hands of men who were not equally yoked (the brothers were not as zealous as they were). That was an opened door to drift off. As the Bible says:

*Do not be deceived: "Evil company corrupts good habits." — 1 Corinthians 15:33*

Be careful of friendship. We will discuss friendship in the next section.

Beloved, the Bible teaches us to run from sin. The devil will come and tempt brothers and sisters ignorant of his devices.

*Or do you not know that he who is joined to a harlot is one body with her? For "the two," He says, "shall become one flesh." 17 But he who is joined to the Lord is one Spirit with Him. 18 Flee sexual immorality. Every sin that a man does is outside the body, but he who commits sexual immorality sins against his own body. — 1 Corinthians 6:16-18*

I strongly suggest brothers and sisters run from any sexual immorality. And if they are tempted, it is important to spend time fasting and praying. You can do this if Jesus could contain himself for 33 years while leading a world ministry. If you are having any sexual temptation, spend time fasting. Pray and ask God to help you in your weakness. Do not let yourself be in positions where you are alone with the opposite sex. Lust is a very atmospheric thing. If you pray and it seems not to change, talk to your pastor or someone higher spiritually. Also, do not connect with others in the church who are living sinful lives. It could worsen the situation as you talk about the issue. It could fuel the problem.

Besides sexual immorality, to keep your holiness, you should run from sexually oriented movies such as porn movies. Do not let any poisoning substance enter your body, for your body is the temple of the Holy Ghost as it is written.

*Or do you not know that your body is the temple of the Holy Spirit who is in you, whom you have from God, and you are not your own? — 1 Corinthians 6:19*

Substances such as alcohol, nicotine, marijuana, and any drug such as heroin, cocaine, etc., should not penetrate your body. Do not be addicted to those. Why would you miss heaven?

*~~ Talk openly to someone higher in the Spirit about your addictions so you can be led through deliverance if needed~~*

*~~Brother and sister, be blameless in all things and maintain a good testimony in your congregation. Try not to have a secret life and be a double-faced saint~~*

*~~Give glory to the name of the Lord living in you~~*

## The Test of the Word

The devil is a liar. He will use lies to tempt you. The devil will always tempt you in three major aspects of your life:

- He will tempt you based on what you already have.
- He will tempt you based on what you know.
- He will tempt you based on what he knows you are looking for.

That is why you ought to be careful. If he dared to tempt our Lord, King Jesus Christ, it is not you that he will spare. But one question remains.

How was Jesus able to overcome the devil? The answer is simple. By the word of God. As the Bible says:

*Then Jesus, filled with the Holy Spirit, returned from the Jordan and was led by the Spirit into the wilderness,* **two** *being tempted for forty days by the devil. And in those days, He ate nothing, and afterward, when they had ended,* **He was hungry.** *3 And the devil said to Him, "If You are the Son of God, command this stone to become bread." 4 But Jesus answered him, saying,* **"It is written,** *'Man shall not live by bread alone, but by every word of God.'" 5 **Then** the devil, taking Him up on a high mountain, showed Him all the kingdoms of the world in a moment of time. 6 And the devil said to Him, "All this authority I will give You, and their glory; for this has been delivered to me, and I give it to whomever I wish. 7 Therefore, if You will worship before me, all will be Yours." 8 And Jesus answered and said to him,* **"Get behind Me, Satan! For it is written,** *'You shall worship the Lord your God, and Him only you shall serve.'" 9 Then he brought Him to Jerusalem, set Him on the pinnacle of the temple, and said to Him, "If You are the Son of God, throw Yourself down from here. 10 For it is written:*

*'He shall give His angels charge over you,*

*To keep you,'*

*11 and, 'In their hands, they shall bear you up,*

*Lest you dash your foot against a stone.'"*

*12 And Jesus answered and said to him,* **"It has been said,** *'You shall not tempt the Lord your God.'" 13 Now when the devil had ended every temptation, he departed from Him until an opportune time. — Luke 4:1-13*

In 13 verses, Jesus replied three times to Satan: "It is written." Why didn't Jesus say, "I call the fire over you"? Or something like, "Die by fire"? Of course, it wouldn't work. Here, Jesus is dealing with Satan, not demons. So, the best way to deal with Satan, the accuser of our brethren, is to use the word back at him as he twists it to push you to rebel against God.

Beloved, it is serious. Many Christians do not read their Bible. They only open it on Sunday while the pastor is preaching. Some people do not even carry it to church with them. Some read it but need help understanding it. Some need to remember what was preached in the Sunday sermon. So, when the enemy comes, he incorrectly uses scripture in the Bible to seduce them. They fall into the trap because there is no foundation in them, no root, no bible knowledge to let them fire back, to counterattack.

Can you imagine? a Christian who has nothing to say to the devil. That is sad.

*~~Beloved brother and sister in Christ, your victory over Satan will depend on how many scriptures you have in your body, soul, and Spirit ~~*

Remember how Adam and Eve fell short of the glory of God in the garden because they could not reply to Satan: "It is written" or "Back off, Satan."

We must all learn from that costly mistake.

*~~People of God, please read the Bible and meditate on it ~~*

In hardship, pain, struggles, and trials, the word of God will keep you going. The word of God is what will give you faith when the enemy attacks from everywhere.

I suggest to all my new converts stepping into the kingdom that they read their Bibles and study them so they may have revelations in the scriptures through the Holy Spirit. When the test of the word comes, be aware that the devil is nearby. It would help if you prepared your spiritual bullets. Have your "it is written" ready to always use. When the devil speaks to you negatively, find a scripture in the Bible that counterattacks what he said.

Beloved, read the word daily, and try to memorize as much scripture as possible.

*~~~Spiritual growth is defined by how much you know; not how much you eat~~~*

## The Test of the Wilderness

Spiritual growth is not only about eating, drinking, laughter, smiles, and joy. Growth combines the above and all difficulties, including time in the wilderness. Growth comes when you pass the tests and learn from them.

As you read the book of Exodus, you see that as soon as the people of Israel left Egypt and went straight into the wilderness, where they spent some 40 years. It is good to notice that nowhere in the Bible before Moses was any prophecy telling the people of Israel they would be tested in the wilderness. I would not argue that God didn't know about it since He knows about everything before it comes to pass.

Do not be fooled. Tests will come with no warning, no revelation, no prophecies. They will just come and surprise you.

The test of the wilderness is the place where:

- You prove your total dependence on God
- Your heart is sanctified and transformed
- Your old nature is killed, giving birth to a new self
- You taste the provision of God
- You count on God alone
- You get to know the ways of God
- You are prepared to receive your blessing
- You are taught to be humble
- You are trained to be obedient to God
- You learn to hear God's voice and recognize the voice of the devil
- God reveals himself to you
- You are led deep into the word of God
- You are drawn into the presence of God in times of difficulties
- You learn to be a mighty fighter
- You see the hand of God every day in everything.

Do not run from the test of the wilderness. Stay away from Egypt like some Israelites did, thinking that Egypt was better than the wilderness, forgetting that after the wilderness, there was a land called Canaan, where honey and milk flowed. As it is written:

*And you shall remember that the Lord your God led you all the way these forty years in the wilderness, to humble you and test you, to know what was in your heart, whether you would keep His commandments or not. 3 So He humbled you, allowed you to hunger, and fed you with manna which you did not know nor did your fathers know, that He might make you know that man shall not live by bread alone; but man lives by every word that proceeds from the mouth of the Lord. 4 Your garments did not wear out on you, nor did your foot swell these forty years. — Deuteronomy 8:2-4*

*~~~Brothers and sisters, the test of wilderness always has an end~~~*

God takes you to the test not to harm you but to elevate you. As tough as it can be, the difference will be clear between a Christian who has gone deep into the wilderness and the one who ran back to Egypt (the world).

You shall be called the son and daughter of light and glory, vases of honor.

*~~~I pray that if you are going through a test if you are in the wilderness, may the Lord God never let your garment be worn out, nor your feet swell~~~.*

Be strong. Be of good courage. Canaan is very close!

**Frustration Test**

The test of frustration is a direct consequence of the test of wilderness. As a new Christian, you will be frustrated at times. You will be frustrated because:

- You may feel like you are behind. Well, life is not a race. Christianity is not a race. Everyone goes at his speed. God blesses everyone in His own Time.
- You may feel like God does not hear your prayers. Yes, God hears your prayers. For even the worst sinner, God hears his prayer of repentance and gives him another chance.
- You may feel like all your efforts lead to nothing and failure. True failure is when you give up. The failure you call failure is called training.
- You may feel like there is no progression in your life and nothing is moving forward. There is a progression in your life; you do not see it since you compare your life to other Christians.

Dear Christian, I went through the test of frustration. I experienced many frustrations. But I committed myself entirely to prayer and fasting in every one of them. As it is written:

*Is anyone among you suffering? Let him pray. Is anyone cheerful? Let him sing psalms. — James 5:13*

Please do not take it out on anyone, even the pastor, whenever you feel frustrated. Many people play the blame game when something is not going right. Ask yourself this question: Why would God allow this? What is the plan of God in permitting this situation? Does God want to teach me something?

You are wising up as you meditate on these questions.

Do not stay away from the assembly of saints when everything is not going great, but instead, pray alone or with your prayer partner.

Beloved precious saints, God does not want us to perish but to live by knowing Him. And some of the best techniques God uses for our growth are tests. They are also a manifestation of His love. God bless you!

*For whom the Lord loves, He chastens,*
*And scourges every son whom He receives. — Hebrews 12:6*

# CHAPTER 6

# FRIENDS AND SPIRITUAL FATHERS

There is so much misunderstanding about spiritual fathers and spiritual mothers. So much controversy is running through the body of Christ on this doctrine. In this chapter, I will bring some important information to end any confusion and help Christians not fall into the trap of deception like many did.

## Spiritual Father/ Spiritual Mother

### Facts about spiritual coverage

Let's consider these general ideas. Any container has a cover, a lid, or a top. Any pan, coffee cup, etc., has a top. Why?

Because without a cover, the contents of the container may spill. If you want to keep the heat, warmth, or coldness of whatever is inside a container, you must cover it. If a container is well covered, you may retain some important qualities of what is inside.

Also, have you ever seen an athlete without a coach? Have you ever seen an athlete without a training ground? Have you ever seen a football player training and teaching himself to defend or attack? Have you ever seen an athlete playing a whole game alone and winning? Have you ever seen a house without a roof? Can you give birth to yourself? Can you baptize yourself (even Jesus needed John the Baptist to get baptized - Luke 3:21)? Can you teach yourself the alphabet, languages, or any skills without being taught by a professor from grade 1 to university? Did you learn to speak by yourself? You learned it through your mother or father. Are you teaching yourself the Bible, or is the Holy Spirit doing it through someone? Can you work in a company without a manager or a boss?

Beloved, there is NO such thing as total independence. You will always depend on someone to go higher. God uses people to bless people. You will always learn from someone. It is a principle God established. You can never make it alone. God prepared and trained people with many experiences and wisdom to impart wisdom to the next generation, just like Moses trained Aaron.

What is an uncontrolled child's behavior like when mom and dad are absent from his life?

Brothers and sisters, let me announce to you that as well as physical orphans, motherless and fatherless, there are also spiritual orphans wandering left and right without mentorship and guidance. That is dangerous for the body of Christ.

**Important facts to never forget.**

God is a blessing, but blessings don't come from heaven like a package shipped to your house. A creature will not travel from heaven to Earth in your living room to give you that blessing. Even if it happened, it would be very seldom, like the case of Mary.

*Now in the sixth month, the angel Gabriel was sent by God to a city of Galilee named Nazareth. — Luke 1:26*

God has a legal and unique way of blessing anyone, whether you are a pastor, prophet, evangelist of men and women, doctor, president, king, minister, worshipper, or any ordinary person. He does it *by using another person.*

*~~~God will always use one person to bless another person. It is principle.~~~*

The book of Proverbs, especially in chapters 1-8, talks about sons hearing the father's instructions.

*Hear, my children, the instruction of a father, and give attention to know understanding. — Proverbs 4:1*

It doesn't only apply to biological sons. It also means spiritual sons.

**Why do you need a spiritual father, a pastor?**

**Or a spiritual coverage to grow?**

First, you need to comprehend that the spiritual world is vast, huge, and very complex, way more complex than our world. The invisible world of demons and the angelic world are complex. You need someone with a deep understanding to explain how it works. You need someone who knows spirituality, has dealt with it, lived in it, and went through it.

Even if you are a person of great knowledge, you will need a master, a mentor, and a father who will help you keep your gift under control. It will save your life and cause no damage to yourself or others. This person will serve as a second opinion in your decision-making. It is someone who has a certain wisdom in life and has made mistakes and learned from them, meaning he has experience. The difference between father and son is not only in age. It is the years of experience in life.

*~~~ Gifts, talents, and skills without wisdom are self-destruction~~~*

The difference between a student and a master is *experience and wisdom,* not skill. You build experience by learning from a master and learning from mistakes.

Therefore:

- You need a spiritual cover to train you in what you don't know because you will never know everything.
- You need a spiritual cover to help you avoid fatal and costly mistakes that can destroy your career. Because your mentor or spiritual father made those mistakes and found a way to escape them. There is a load of knowledge gained to be transferred to the next generation.
- You need a spiritual father to help you pass through places where he failed by teaching you tricks.
- You need a spiritual father because you want to prolong your life and career.
- You need a spiritual cover to help in tough times and to pray for you. In spirituality, there are many levels (high, higher, and highest), and you need someone who has a higher level than you to save you.
- You need a spiritual cover to speak words over you.

~~~ *Only a good swimmer can save a drowning person* ~~~

**How do you know that a pastor is your spiritual father?**

- Does he show deep concern about your life and problems?
- Does he seem to care about you as a person?
- Does he spend time teaching you?
- Does he correct or rebuke you when you make mistakes?
- Does he invest in you by sharing his experiences and knowledge?
- Do you relate to him?
- Do you feel connected to him? There should be an unexplainable feeling between your spiritual father/mother and you that makes you never want to leave while remaining loyal and faithful to him, even if you both are experiencing differences.
- Are you protective of him?
- Do you love him?
- Does he love you?
- Do you believe and support his vision?
- Do you learn from him?

- Do you feel challenged and pushed to do better than him?
- Does God reveal your life to him?
- Does he cover you spiritually and fight for you?
- Does he inspire you? Better yet, do you want to look like him?
- Do you want his anointing or his gift?
- Do you want to be used by God like him?
- Do you want to flow under the anointing like him?
- Does he appear in your dreams as often as possible to talk with you, to help fight spiritual battles?
- Do you trust him?
- Does he trust you?

In my own experience, God used the face of my spiritual father to speak to me at very important moments of my life.

- Does he push you or coach you into your calling?
- Did God tell you he is your spiritual father? If God told you so, do not return a while later and say the same. God says you are not my father anymore. I have seen that so many times. As you can't deny your biological father, you can't deny your spiritual father.
- Does your spiritual father secretly pray for you when you need it?
- Do you care about him and show deep respect and honor to his anointing, mantle, and ministry?
- Do you feel ashamed when you speak about him to people? If yes, it is better to sit and talk with him.
- Do you feel ashamed to present him even if he has a handicap, an accent, or a complexion?
- Do you speak positively about him in public?
- Do you treat his wife and his family members like your own?
- Do you feel part of his biological family, even if you are from a different country, race, or gender?
- Do you serve him faithfully?

**Special remarks:**

- God cares about your soul and is ready to do anything to save it. So, you could achieve your destiny and prosper. In that case, he will send you a spiritual father, a mentor, or a coach to lead you to green pastures and do what your biological parents sometimes failed to do.
- There are four types of education. There is parental *education*; it is usually messed up because of broken homes and abusive parents. *Life education* usually makes people bitter because of the wicked and mean people they meet. *School education* doesn't teach you moral values but theoretical knowledge to pass classes and graduate. And lastly, *spiritual (church) education* is offered by the Lord through churches and pastors. It is the most important because it encompasses the other three. When parents fail, life hardships negatively transform people, and church (kingdom education) education takes over to better people when school education fails.
- It is true that just like some biological fathers, spiritual fathers could mess up the calling to watch over God's sheep and souls. I strongly suggest that every Christian pray that God sends them a good spiritual father who will lead them straight into their destiny.

**Example of spiritual coverage in the Bible**

**Joshua & Moses:**

*After the death of Moses the servant of the Lord, it came to pass that the Lord spoke to Joshua the son of Nun, Moses' assistant, saying: "Moses My servant is dead. Now therefore, arise, go over this Jordan, you and all this people, to the land which I am giving to them—the children of Israel. Every place that the sole of your foot will tread upon I have given you, as I said to Moses."—Joshua 1:1-3*

*Then the Lord said to Moses, "Behold, the days approach when you must die; call Joshua, and present yourselves in the tabernacle of meeting, that*

*I may inaugurate (to commission) him. "So, Moses and Joshua went and presented themselves in the tabernacle of meeting. Now the Lord appeared at the tabernacle in a pillar of cloud, and the pillar of cloud stood above the door of the tabernacle. — Deuteronomy 31:14-15*

*So, Moses arose with his assistant (Servant) Joshua, and Moses went up to the mountain of God. — Exodus 24:13*

*So, the Lord spoke to Moses face to face, as a man speaks to his friend. And he would return to the camp, but his servant Joshua the son of Nun, a young man, did not depart from the tabernacle. — Exodus 33:11*

**Elijah & Elisha:**

*So, he departed from there, and found Elisha, the son of Shaphat, who was plowing with twelve yokes of oxen before him, and he was with the twelfth. Then Elijah passed by him and threw his mantle on him. And he left the oxen and ran after Elijah and said, "Please let me kiss my father and my mother, and then I will follow you." And he said to him, "Go back again, for what have I done to you?" — 1 Kings 19:19-20*

*Also, you shall anoint Jehu, the son of Nimshi as king over Israel. And Elisha, the son of Shaphat of Abel Meholah, you shall anoint as prophet in your place. — 1 Kings 19:16*

*(Elisha fellows Elijah even though he told him to stay back so he can receive a double portion of the anointing.) — 2 Kings 2:1-25*

*But Jehoshaphat said, "Is there no prophet of the Lord here, that we may inquire of the Lord by him?" So one of the servants of the king of Israel answered and said, "Elisha, the son of Shaphat, is here, who poured water on the hands of Elijah." — 2 Kings 3:11*

***Even Elisha had a servant:***

*But Gehazi, the servant of Elisha, the man of God. — 2 Kings 5:20*

**Jesus & the disciples:**

*And when He had called His twelve disciples to Him, He gave them power over unclean spirits, to cast them out, and to heal all kinds of sickness and all kinds of disease. Now the names of the twelve apostles are these: first, Simon, who is called Peter, and Andrew his brother; James the son of Zebedee, and John his brother; Philip and Bartholomew; Thomas and Matthew the tax collector; James the son of Alphaeus, and Lebbaeus, whose surname was Thaddaeus; Simon the Canaanite, and Judas Iscariot, who also betrayed Him.*
*— Matthew 10:1-4*

**Paul & Ananias:**

*And Ananias went his way and entered the house; and laying his hands on him, he said, "Brother Saul, the Lord Jesus, who appeared to you on the road as you came, has sent me that you may receive your sight and be filled with the Holy Spirit." Immediately, there fell from his eyes something like scales, and he received his sight at once, and he arose and was baptized. — Acts 9:17-18*

**Paul & Timothy:**

*To_Timothy, a true son in the faith: Grace, mercy, and peace from God our Father and Jesus Christ our Lord. — 1 Timothy 1:2*

*You, therefore, my son, be strong in the grace that is in Christ Jesus. And the things that you have heard from me among many witnesses commit these to faithful men who will be able to teach others also. — 2 Timothy 2:1-2*

**Important Information:**

*Imitate me, just as I also imitate Christ. Now I praise you, brethren, that you remember me in all things and keep the traditions just as I delivered them to you. — 1 Corinthians 11:1-2*

- You can always get the anointing through someone else. It is called "impartation."

*~~ Anointing always copies a model ~~*

- You will remain at a low spiritual level if you do not connect to a higher anointing stream.
- Everything explained above also applies to the concept of a spiritual mother. There is little difference between a spiritual mother and a spiritual father except for gender.

**Seek a mentor.**

The concept of spiritual father and mother is misunderstood, and many people do not want a pastor who knows their business. Everybody has a different level of trust.

In the case you do not trust anybody, you have the option to choose a mentor . You can have a mentor in finances, relationships, marriage, spirituality, sports, education, etc.

Mentorship deals with a very specific domain of life. You could have a spiritual father and mentors because a spiritual father does not know everything. He is human like you with the grace of God upon him. A spiritual father remains a spiritual father as long as he lives because it is a covenant, and covenants are not easily broken, but mentorships could be temporary. Either way, both are very important.

I have a spiritual father. He is the one who trained, groomed, and sent me into ministry. I honor his anointing and his position as a father. However, I also have some mentors. They are experienced and trusted advisers. They mentor me in specific areas of my life and my ministry. I have access to them and ask questions as often as possible. It is for the glory of God.

Going by the principle of blessing, if you do not want to have a spiritual father because of such and such reasons, please connect with a mentor. Life is complicated in general. Spiritual life can be complex as well. You must make it with someone. Connect with someone who will teach you constantly and transfer their wisdom to you.

To my fellow Christians, if you know that you have a calling, if you know that sooner or later you will be serving God, pray for God to connect you to a God-fearing man of God for your training. You cannot be a spiritual orphan. Please connect with a genuine man of God so you can go through serious ministry training. Find yourself a cover.

**Good friends, prayer partners**

You are not entitled to be friends with everybody or anybody. However, here is another extremely important ingredient you surely need to succeed in Christian life. You will need a good friend, someone who can be your confidant, a person who can be more than your biological brother.

*A friend loves at all times, And a brother is born for adversity. — Proverbs 17:17*

Yes, you need that friend who loves you unconditionally, who becomes like a brother in times of adversity, loves you dearly, and knits to your soul. I call it a covenant brother or a covenant sister.

The Bible says:

*Now, when he had finished speaking to Saul, the soul of Jonathan was knit to the soul of David, and Jonathan loved him as his own soul. Saul took him that day and would not let him go home to his father's house anymore. Then Jonathan and David made a covenant because he loved him as his own soul. And Jonathan took off the robe that was on him and gave it to David, with his armor, even to his sword and his bow and his belt. — 1 Samuel 18:1-4*

It would be best if you had a friend like Jonathan. A friend who will introduce you to kings. One who will not mind sharing his meal with you and will not mind giving you his robe. He will not mind fighting for you. He will not mind putting his life in danger to save you from distress. He will be a friend in good times and bad. Like they say: "He's got your back!"

Your Christian friend must be loyal. He must be your confidant.

Here are some descriptions of what your Christian best friend should look like:

- They must be unique. There is one David for only one Jonathan.
- They must love you unconditionally
- They are connected to you for life, no matter the distance
- They trust you
- They are ready to share what they have with you
- They are in it for the long haul. If you go down, they go down; if you go up, they do too.
- If you are in jail, they will see you
- If you get in trouble, they will get in trouble with you
- They will meet you at the crack house, in the pits of hell, or at the hospital
- They are there for you, and they are with you
- They are there to make sure that you will enter your destiny
- Without them, you will never see what God called you to be
- They will tell you when you are wrong
- They will not lie to you. They will tell you the real truth about everything.
- They will give you their real opinion when you ask them
- They are real
- What they say behind your back is what they will say in front of you
- They will do anything for you without expecting anything in return
- They will not mind fasting days and nights for you
- They will not mind praying for you
- They will not mind praying with you

If you meet a good friend who fits all these criteria, do not let them go. Do all it takes to keep them. It is a friendship that lasts forever. They will surely be important to fulfill your destiny.

**My personal story:**

Right after the New Year's celebration in 2000, I rededicated my life to the Lord. I started going to church. It did not take me too long to be very engaged in church activities. My fire and my zeal were both at the highest point. I couldn't stay still. I wanted to do anything for the Lord. I started discovering my spiritual gift. However, there were many spiritual things I needed help understanding or explaining. The general overseer of my home church was too busy because there were many people to pray for. I had to find a way to keep my fire up so it would not die through hard times. I had to find a good friend with a strong relationship with the Lord to help me stand up when I am weak or fall. As the Bible says:

*Two are better than one because they have a good reward for their labor.*

*For if they fall, one will lift up his companion. But woe to him who is alone when he falls, for he has no one to help him up. — Ecclesiastes 4:9-10*

In churches, I have seen some religious people who lack so much wisdom that they turn their mouths against the pastor, the first lady, and anyone in the congregation. They criticize almost everything. They always have a bad view of anything in the church. You do not want to be around these kinds of people. They will mess up your mind, putting things in your mind.

My friend's name was Marcelin Digbe. He was a very straightforward friend. Prayer and fasting were his habits. He was honest and the type of friend I would tell my deepest secret, knowing he would never spit it out to anyone. He is a confidant. Beloved, you need a friend like that. We are still friends today despite the distance. He lives in the Ivory Coast, my home country. He still prays and fasts for me, and vice versa. Countless times, he has supported me. Whenever he calls me, I try to be there for him. The Lord has revealed things about me to him that I completely ignored. That has saved my life on many occasions. We may have differences and disagreements, but they do not last long—glory to God. I pray the Lord sends you a faithful friend.

**What is a church? Why do you need a church? What is a good church? How can I find a good church?**

We have so much to say when it comes to church. This section is extremely important. I will provide key elements to help your growth. I will state some facts most people do not discuss for fear of exposing their practices. First, we want to look into the definition of a church. What is a church, according to God's vision for humanity?

*1- What is Church?*

The church represents the body of Christ,

*Now, you are the body of Christ and members of the individual. — 1 Corinthians 12:27*

It is all the believers, the assembly of saints. The church is the family of saints on Earth, representing and manifesting the kingdom of God on Earth with the help of the Holy Spirit.

*God is great to be feared in the assembly of the saints and to be held in reverence by all those around Him. — Psalm 89:7*

The church is those who are saved by the ultimate sacrifice of Christ on the cross through faith. It has nothing to do with the building. The building would be called "a synagogue." Nowadays, we confuse the building with the church. We can, therefore, say that you can create a church at your house with some members of the body of Christ, though you are not alone. Church has nothing to do with the denomination, the church's name, the building's size, or how wealthy the people are.

The church does not belong to anybody, not even the pastor. The pastor is just the manager. But it belongs to Jesus Christ. No one can claim ownership. Jesus is the chief of the church.

*And I also say to you that you are Peter, and on this rock, I will build **My church**, and the gates of Hades shall not prevail against it. — Matthew 16:18*

Notice that Jesus said, I will build my church. Jesus built his church because he is a great architect, knowing that he who builds a building surely has the means to complete the work. Jesus is automatically the owner of the church. Let no spiritual leader or Christian forget about that. The church is the embassy of heaven on Earth. When God wants to rule the church, it happens through you. He empowers you through the church and the teachings of the kingdom. The church is the open gate of heaven on Earth, where angels take up our prayers and return them with blessings.

You alone cannot constitute the church of Christ, but you alone are a member of the church of Christ or a member of the body of Christ. However, you can have a personal relationship or communion with God, Jesus, and the Holy Spirit.

**2- Why do you need a church**

We have defined and explained a church. Now, I need to explain why it is important for a Christian to be at church.

Remember, Jesus said:

*And I also say to you that you are Peter, and on this rock, I will build **My church**, and the gates of Hades shall not prevail against it. — Matthew 16:18.*

Jesus will build a church so strong, powerful, and anointed. The church will be built not on sand but on the rock of ages, Jesus Christ himself. The gates of hell will never prevail against his church. This means that the church of Jesus will be equipped with such authority and power that even the most powerful satanic entity will never prevail against it. Hell is so weak before the church. Hell is where unbelievers, sinners, and outlaws, including Satan and his demons, will be eternally after the rapture. Hell is also pain and suffering without Jesus. Hell is every problem Satan brings on Earth to destabilize the world. The church will be so great and strong that it will have answers to every problem that humanity faces. The church will even be able to open the iron gates of hell and empty out its occupants. Jesus and the church will forever have the keys to hell, and death will no longer have control over the children of God. Beloved, we have no idea of the power of the church of Jesus Christ. He paid a price at the cross to break the power of hell and sin over the church. That is why the Bible says:

*O Death, where is your sting?*
*O Hades, where is your victory? The sting of death is sin, and the strength of*
*sin is the law. — 1 Corinthians 15:55-56*

I was asked once by a religious leader, "Why do Christians pray so much and not do anything?" I replied: If Christians stop praying, expect a third world war the next day. The presence of all the saints worshipping, singing, praising, praying, and serving Jesus brings peace and the glory of God to the globe.

That is why I strongly suggest that anybody, particularly newborn Christians who want to last long in their Christian journey, be an active church member of Christ. An active church member is one God uses to stand against the gates of hell and destroy the works of the devil. He is the one that God can use to provide answers to the tough problems that humanity faces. You must be part of this powerful spiritual organization led by Jesus Christ. Regardless of how many bad things happen in the church of Christ today, it is still Christ's private property. Human beings are not always perfect.

I was sometimes asked if it is necessary to go to church to make it to heaven, to be blessed, and to grow. Here is my answer.

To make it to heaven, Jesus decides, based on your relationship with Him. If you have made Jesus your savior and repented from sin, you are part of the body of Christ (the church). Your salvation is guaranteed. Do not hide behind the church as a physical entity (the building); live an unholy life and expect to make it to heaven. That is why you must work at your salvation. The building itself will not save you, however, it is the building owner who saves you.

A good church is full of the anointing of God to break every yoke. When the children of God are gathered, Satan flees. God releases his supernatural power, and traffic between heaven and Earth flows. Prayers go up, and blessings come down. I have said it many times: When Christians get together for the glory of God, all kinds of blessings rain down. So, yes, it is very important to go to church (as a physical entity) to be blessed. I have seen the manifestation of the blessing of God (healing, marriage, breakthrough, peace, etc.) in a congregation. A good church where Jesus is the chief, where the Holy Spirit has His way, is always a good place to grow.

*So then neither he who plants is anything, nor he who waters, but God who gives the increase. — 1 Corinthians 3:7*

God gives the increase. It is God that pushes you to growth. He will make you grow. So, come on, do not be selfish. Get up and join a church.

Amen!

### 3- What is a good Church?

We explained above why you need a church to grow. You may be wondering what a good church is. That is a very legitimate question. We are in the 21st century and have seen all types of doctrine. It is not the right place and time to talk about this now. But so much evil has been done in the churches that most new Christians hesitate to join. Some people look for a good sign or clues to join a church. I will tell you that it is not easy, but all things are possible with God. In this section, I will give some clues or signs to look for as you look for a good church to attend. Your future depends on this.

1. A good church has nothing to do with the beauty of the building, the quality of the sound system, nice decorations, etc.
2. A good church is not based on the age, race, or gender of the spiritual leader.
3. A good church has nothing to do with the geographical location: on the mountain, in a valley, in the sand, or in water.
4. A good church always preaches and focuses on Jesus and the message of the cross.
5. A good church lays the foundation of grace and exposes sin while offering a pathway for sinners to repent.

6. A good church is a Holy Ghost-filled church.
7. A good church is a church that is based on the word of God and preaches it, teaches it, and believes in it.
8. A good church uses no other book than the Bible (66 books from Genesis to Revelation).
9. A good church doesn't deny the doctrine of baptism of water, spirit, and fire.
10. A good church does not reject the manifestation of the gifts of the spirit.
11. Jesus is the owner and the first person of the church, not the pastor.
12. A good church is not money-oriented.
13. A good church promotes social welfare. It helps people experiencing poverty, those in need, widows, and orphans.
14. A good church doesn't let the world dominate its faith in God.
15. A good church is welcoming, embraces everyone, and does not discriminate.
16. A good church is a training ground.
17. A good church equips the saint for the work of God.
18. A good church is a place for believers to discover their gifts and use them to change the world.
19. A good church is a very influential church in the community.

## 4- How can I find a good church?

Though I gave 19 signs to look for in a good church, every church could differ for many reasons. Every Christian seems to have different tastes when it comes to church. Some Christians love churches that have a great praise and worship team. Others prefer a church that is based mainly on deliverance and healing.

# CHAPTER 7

# OTHER HELPFUL ELEMENTS

As I write this book, I want to ensure that I include every piece of information and every tip necessary for your total growth for the glory of God. I want to make sure that everything is noticed. Read and apply what you read. I can guarantee you that your spiritual life will be very inspirational.

In this last chapter, I will highlight some important elements to look out for.

## Love others

You will always deal with people if you are on Earth. God will use people to bless you. He will also use people to shape you. You'd better get ready. The enemies will attack through people. You will need to practice love. You will need to develop this fruit of the Spirit; otherwise, you will be bitter and hateful, unable to let go of what people did to you in the past while serving God in the church. They say:

*~~~ Kill them with love ~~~*

Love disarms evildoers. Love shows that you are a child of God. Love demonstrates how much you are transformed into a clean image of Christ Jesus.

*By this, all will know that you are My disciples if you have a love for one another.* — *John 13:35*

**Be kind and serve others.**

You cannot love without being kind to one another. David said:

*Now David said, "Is there still anyone who is left of the house of Saul, that I may show him kindness for Jonathan's sake?"* — *2 Samuel 9:1*

Show kindness to people like David did. David had just become king and returned to offer kindness to his former enemy. Let your kindness be known in the church. Never stop helping people, even though you may get evil in return. God records every good deed and one day, God will return it to you in many ways. The body of Christ is sick of evil. Be an exception and an example before God, the angels, demons, and humankind. Whatever people ask of you, do it if you have the ability. By being kind to others, you are serving them. To become a good leader, you ought to serve people well.

**Talk about God, evangelize, spread the gospel.**

As you read the gospels, there are many times when Jesus would heal someone and tell them not to tell anybody what happened. But because of the tremendous and overwhelming joy, they spread the news. They let people know what the Lord had done for them. In doing so, they became preachers of the gospel. They spread the good news of Jesus, our savior king, and many people believed in Jesus. Brothers and sisters, if the Lord healed you or delivered you from any bondage, spread the news.

Do not hide it. Let people know what God did for you. Invite them to church. Evangelize, and do not be ashamed of what you have become by the power of the Holy Ghost. Many Christians hide their faith when they are among unbelievers. Please talk about Jesus. The more you talk about God, the more your spiritual gifts grow. God uses bold people. Be a little evangelist, even though you are not ordained. Prove yourself in these small things, and God will entrust you with greater things. Try to preach first to your close family and close friends. Let them know about Christ.

Preach also to your classmates and coworkers. Do not stop even if you are mocked. Do not stop even if you are laughed at. Do not stop even if you are rejected and humiliated. I pray the Holy Spirit helps you in the task. Your reward will be great!

**Watch your character and seek transformation and change of character.**

The good thing about church is that church is a good place for God to reshape your character. Your anointing will bring people around you, but your character will keep them around you. When you are newly converted and begin attending church, you are not expected to be perfect. However, you cannot remain as you came. God will start working on you through his word, from the inside to the outside. Allow God to transform you. Allow God to remove your pride and put humility in you. You must learn to develop the fruit of the Spirit in you: *"love, joy, peace, longsuffering, kindness, goodness, faithfulness, gentleness, self-control."* — *Galatians 5:22-23*

As you can tell, if a newborn grows, it is easy to detect a growing Christian. Their words are full of wisdom; their characters are simple, meek, and easy. They are always happy no matter what. They are easily approachable and have a good reputation. It is visible.

*When I was a child, I spoke as a child, I understood as a child, I thought as a child; but when I became a man, I put away childish things.* — *1 Corinthians 13:11*

Beloved, let's not be fooled; Christians with good character in a church will always have fewer skirmishes and less conflict with others. People will gather around them more often. Just watch your behavior. Let the Holy Spirit work on you.

**Never partake in any strife and drama in a church.**

I always say a church is a gathering of sick individuals seeking a better life and future. So, it is not uncommon to see two sick folks getting into a fight. It could be a small disagreement solvable in one minute or as huge as a tornado. The consequences could be disastrous to the point of dividing the church or scattering the sheep.

Jesus said:

*"Woe to the world because of offenses! For offenses must come, but woe to that man by whom the offense comes."* — *Matthew 18:7*

So, it is normal for offenses, dramas, and scandals to come, but he who caused them bears the consequences. The Lord condemns the guilty, and he clears the innocent. He is the God of justice.

If a situation occurs at church, it is advised to keep your mouth shut if you are not directly concerned. Otherwise, address your concerns to the pastor or leader politely. Above all, pray about the situation. Make some supplication to the Lord so that the situation will not escalate to damaging the church. God will bless you for that. Do not poison your Spirit by listening to gossipers in the church. Some people talk about everything, saying and extrapolating everything. I beg you, do not be their friend. Do not pick these individuals as friends because they do not keep secrets. In a church, it is easy to be blessed; do not do what can attract a curse over you. It is as simple as drinking water. Do not go against the head of the church and his wife. Be more of a peacemaker than a divisive Christian. Remember, it is written: *"Touch not my anointed one"* — *Psalms 105:15*.

It is an unpardonable mistake many Christians make, and they then face bad consequences.

Do not be rebellious. Do not associate with rebels. Do not walk among the scornful. As the Bible says:

*Blessed is the man who walks not in the counsel of the ungodly, nor stands in the path of sinners, nor sits in the seat of the scornful.* — *Psalms 1:1*

**Learn to be a leader, not a controller.**

Take some leadership classes. These will be highly necessary in the future. As a new Christian seeking growth opportunity, do not seek to impose your ideas and opinions on your leader or the visionary of the church. Let everything you do or suggest align with the church's vision. If the things you suggested are not considered, there is no need to be frustrated. Most Christians are frustrated at church when things are not moving fast enough or not going the way they wish they would go. Be patient and act wise. If you see something that you think should be corrected, voice it respectfully to the upper leaders. Remember, growth comes through learning. Suck in the lessons and teachings. Learn from others' mistakes and your own mistakes. Learn from your pastor and your spiritual father. God is preparing you to be a world changer.

**Never be too busy with your activities to the point of forgetting your duties at church.**

As a pastor, I have seen all types of scenarios in the body of Christ. One of the saddest cases is when I see a very determined, engaged brother or sister serving in the church with fire and joy, and one day, I do not see them serving as they used to. You do not see them at church as you used to. You do not feel their fire as you used to. There is no longer joy in their service before the Lord.

What happened? What went wrong? What happened is that most Christians have needs to meet. Jobs, money, rent, car payments, family, and marriages take attention. As they serve God, they have another part of their mind thinking and worrying. It becomes their weakness. The devil knows it. Since he knows it, he starts to press on it. He intensifies his attacks. The Christian serves God but in worry. He has many questions in his mind. I am serving God, but how and when will I get married? How am I going to pay my bills? Can I have a better job? I want more money to pay my bills and pick up extra hours at work. I must have a second job to make more money. The worries are increasing, and the strong desire to please God is diminishing. This is a very strong weapon of Satan in these last days to discourage Christians and weaken the church.

What can you do when you are facing such challenges?

- You must know what the Bible says about worry:

*Be anxious for nothing, but in everything by prayer and supplication, with thanksgiving, let your requests be made known to God. — Philippians 4:6*

The Bible says to pray over everything. Let God know about the issues before you let men know.

*Which of you, by worrying, can add one cubit to his stature? — Matthew 6:27*

If a situation of job or bill appears while you are serving, do not lose control. Keep calm. Do not leave the service of God to take care of your own business. It is a very bad decision.

- Have faith in God. You must believe that He who called you for His service will care for you. Regardless of the type of job you are applying for, never let it overtake your service and attendance at church. Refuse to work at any cost on Sundays.

*Then Peter began to say to Him, "See, we have left all and followed You." So Jesus answered and said, "Assuredly, I say to you, there is no one who has left house or brothers or sisters or father or mother or wife or children or lands, for My sake and the gospel's, who shall not receive a hundredfold now in this time—houses and brothers and sisters and mothers and children and lands, with persecutions—and in the age to come, eternal life. 31 But many who are first will be last, and the last first." — Mark 10:28-31*

- If you have a busy work schedule, ask friends or the intercessory team to support you in prayer so God can change your schedule to attend weekly and Sunday services.

**Have bible study in your DNA.**

The pastor cannot teach and peach everything during Sunday Service. During Sunday service, you cannot interrupt the preaching and ask questions. All you can do is shout amen! Bible study is a good platform for listening and asking questions.

I love bible studies. I suggest to Christians who want to grow to make Bible study their hobby. If there is no bible study day at your church, attend a group study. Try to meet with friends to share the word and pray. Let someone responsible be the leader of the group. He must report to the head pastor at every bible study meeting. Get the word of God in you to the maximum. It will help you in tough times.

**Don't play with your holy life and "sanctification."**

Sanctification means to be set apart. If you want to please God, you must long for the nature of God, that is, "holiness." Run from any sin. Even if anyone at church is living a double life, being a Christian on Sunday and a partier on the weekend, do not copy them. Be a genuine believer with no blemish and no double life. Run away from friends who are negative influences and lead you astray. The Bible says:

*Do not be deceived: "Evil company corrupts good habits." — 1 Corinthians 15:33*

*Flee sexual immorality. Every sin that a man does is outside the body, but he who commits sexual immorality sins against his own body. — 1 Corinthians 6:18*

The Bible is clear on these things. God will use you for greater things. He will send you worldwide to minister, but you must watch over your testimony and reputation to be accepted by people. Remember, sin closes doors and shatters blessings. Let your lifestyle be sanctified, and God will reward you.

**Know your weaknesses.**

No one is perfect. Everyone has his weaknesses. Having weaknesses is one thing but knowing them is another thing. Once you can detect your weaknesses, ask God's grace to overcome them. Pray that the devil will not use your weak point to bring you down. Pray and fast, asking God to support you in your weakness. He is faithful, and His goodness endures forever. God will never let you perish.

*Watch and pray, lest you enter into temptation. The Spirit, indeed is willing, but the flesh is weak. — Matthew 26:41*
Yes, indeed, the flesh is weak. That is why you want to deal with it in fasting and prayer.

**Be vigilant like a snake; watch out for potential danger.**

Carelessness is a sin. It only helps a little if you want to become great. I am not saying you must care about everything but be vigilant and watchful.

The Bible says:

*A prudent man foresees evil and hides himself;*
*They simply pass on and are punished. — Proverbs 27:12*

To be prudent is to act carefully when you see something fishy or that does not look right. Take another route. Or, in other words, run from it. Jesus instructs us to be vigilant. Be wary of fake friends and fake people. Be wary of people who preach you a different gospel from the real gospel of Jesus. Be careful of pastors preaching heresy. Be careful of fake prophets telling you what God says, but God didn't say anything. Be careful of fake unbiblical doctrines justifying and legalizing human malpractices. Be careful not to be led by the Spirit of Judas that betrayed Jesus. Be smart by not considering yourself as better than anybody and remain humble in all your ways. There is danger everywhere. God will make you see it. He will warn you, but it is up to you to walk carefully so as not to fall into the trap of the ungodly. Be careful of seduction. The devil will try to seduce you by presenting a fake blessing (a copy of what the Lord has prepared for you). Be vigilant and have discernment.

**Never sit with gossipers and slanders.**

This is an interesting point. It is a killing disease in all churches, regardless of the type of church and denomination. Gossip and slander a church breaker. My advice for newborn Christians making their first steps in the kingdom is to never participate in gossip or slander. Let people say whatever they want to say, but as far as you are concerned, be careful when voicing your opinion if a problem occurs; as disastrous as it could be, never be the one to spray evil smell around.

Do not give heed to some individuals' negative opinions. It could affect and infect your peace of mind. Never sit with gossipers. If you go to a place where people are exposing secrets and talking badly about members in a church, remain quiet, avoid the topic, or leave. They will have their reward before Jesus comes back. Do not let anyone speak badly about the pastor or his wife. Even if they are wrong, they are your spiritual parents. If you are asked a question that pushes you to talk in a gossiping way, answer: I am not part of it! Next time, you will not be questioned again. If you know how to keep your mouth under control, you will save your life. You will receive blessings above blessings. You will build trust and consideration with people. You will be an incomparable leader, a faithful disciple. Talk less and pray more for the issues to be fixed. Gossipers never do anything but talk. They never pray and fast to see change, but they murmur. Please, mind your own life and stay focused. Whatever doesn't concern you, do not let it waste your time. May God help you. Amen!

*You shall not circulate a false report. Do not put your hand with the wicked to be an unrighteous witness. — Exodus 23:1*

*For I am afraid that when I come, I may not find you as I want you to be, and you may not find me as you want me to be. I fear that there may be discord, jealousy, fits of rage, selfish ambition, **slander, gossip**, arrogance, and disorder. — 2 Corinthians 12:20*

**Participate in seminars and conferences.**

*My people are destroyed for lack of knowledge because you have rejected knowledge, I also will reject you from being priest for Me; Because you have forgotten the law of your God, I also will forget your children. — Hosea 4:6.*

The devil will use your lack of knowledge to bring you down. Remember, what you do not know is what can kill you. Knowledge is the key. Ignorance is a curse. To die ignorant is to die unachieved and unfulfilled. I rebuke ignorance in your life in the name of Jesus Christ. I strongly suggest that Christians participate in any seminar. Go to seminars as often as possible, as much as you can, whether leadership seminars, prayer meetings, or kingdom mentality seminars. Any Christian seminar you can find interesting and spiritually nourishing, go for it. Take notes and apply these notes to your life. As you go to conferences, you will collect revelations or key information you might not have learned at church. That is a plus for your Christian life. You could share that new knowledge with your friends, and you will become a great blessing to the body of Christ. In addition, if you can attend a bible school, bible college, or Christian university, please go for it. Listen to tapes and videos of other teaching and preaching. Widen your spectrum of information.

*~~~~ The more you learn, the more you grow~~~~*

**Seek spiritual experience with the Holy Ghost.**

Someone once said: "Until you meet Jesus personally, you can never be saved." That statement is true, for no one has ever met Jesus and remained the same. In the Bible, whenever anyone goes to the master or if the master goes to them, something happens. It is a life-changing experience to meet Jesus. God is a hiding God. He hides so you can seek him. Brothers and sisters, seek God more than you seek success. He said:

*And you will seek Me and find Me when you search for Me with all your heart. 14 I will be found by you, says the Lord, and I will bring you back from your captivity; I will gather you from all the nations and from all the places where*

*I have driven you, says the Lord, and I will bring you to the place from which I cause you to be carried away captive. — Jeremiah 29:13-14*

Spiritual experiences are unforgettable. You can never remove them from your mind. When you become Christian, you receive a first measure of anointing and power that makes you speak in tongues or have a couple of dreams here and there. Maybe you can give a couple of Prophetic words, hear God's word, or preach a message. You may be able to lead a prayer group, maybe open a church. However, there will be times when you feel stagnant. You know inside of you that there is more. There is more to take in, there is more to swallow, there is more to see. The first level is fading away. You must go to the next level. You know there is a substance you need to get, and it is as if you cannot explain it; no one can understand you. It is exactly at that time that seeking a spiritual encounter is critical. If you do not do so, you end up drying out. Moses would always go to the mountain to receive instructions on how to lead and guide the people. He would receive instruction about constructing the temple of God and the ark of covenant. Sometimes, it may require taking a seven, 10, 12, 21, or even 40-day fast. It will require you to pay a heavy price to go to the next level. You must have a personal encounter with Jesus. You must meet Jesus personally. Jesus wants to show himself, but you must seek him first.

**~~Be mindful of this, and do not be spiritually stagnant. Seek a divine encounter. ~~**

# CONCLUSION

After reading this book, we hope you have been blessed and enlightened about spiritual growth in your local church. It will help you to make the most of your journey with the Lord Jesus Christ. Never forget what the bible says:

*And the things that you have heard from me among many witnesses commit these to faithful men who will be able to teach others also. — 2 Timothy 2:2*

All that you have read and learned from me in this book will be useless if you do not put it into practice and teach it to other new members of the church.

Bear in mind, dear friend, that although you have accepted the Lord as your savior and deliverer, you must dedicate yourself to the learning process of growth. The process may seem lengthy and slow, but your commitment will turn it into an interesting journey. You must understand that growth is not a matter of your capability and ability alone. The Holy Spirit will water the seed, and growth will proceed. The enemy will arise as he usually does, but you should know you are more than an overcomer. As it is written:

*Yet in all these things, we are more than conquerors through Him who loved us. — Romans 8:37*

God wants you to go from call to choose. It will not happen overnight, but you must believe in God and yourself. God loves you, and He does not want to perish. This is why He inspired me to write this book full of steps. After completion, God's mighty, raw power will flow over you. God will send you to the next level because you have built a good foundation.

*~~ **God bless you** ~~*
*Enjoy!*

# ABOUT THE AUTHOR

Evangelist Pastor Eric Kouassi loves Jesus Christ, the living God. Born in the Ivory Coast, he served God early and has been preaching the Gospel for over 20 years. He specializes in deliverance, healing, and revival ministries. He founded LEVI LLC to render professional and leadership training services. He also hosts the "Kingdom with No Limit" TV Show.

Evangelist Eric Kouassi has pastored the Overcomers Ministry Church branch in Omaha, Nebraska, since February 2013.

Evangelist Pastor Eric Kouassi loves Jesus Christ, the living God. Born in the Ivory Coast, he served God early and has been preaching the Gospel for over 20 years. He specializes in deliverance, healing, and revival ministries. He founded LEVI LLC to render professional and leadership training services. He also hosts the "Kingdom with No Limit" TV Show.

Evangelist Eric Kouassi has pastored the Overcomers Ministry Church branch in Omaha, Nebraska, since February 2013.

Printed in the United States
by Baker & Taylor Publisher Services

Printed in the United States
by Baker & Taylor Publisher Services